ABC

Read to Me!

Teaching Letter of the Week in the Library & Classroom

Toni Buzzeo

UpstartBooks™

Janesville, Wisconsin

To Marge Miller and Carol Snitger, who always asked me to
share Dawdle Duckling when it was "Y" week!

Published by UpstartBooks
401 South Wright Road
Janesville, Wisconsin 53547
1-800-448-4887

Copyright © 2009 by Toni Buzzeo

The paper used in this publication meets the minimum requirements of American National
Standard for Information Science — Permanence of Paper for Printed Library Material.
ANSI/NISO Z39.48-1992.

ABC Read to Me!

Table of Contents

ABC Read to Me!

Introduction

Many of us know "Letter of the Week" as a long-standing approach to early literacy introduction in our schools at the preschool and Kindergarten levels. Using this method, we take an incremental approach to the alphabet and its sounds, adding new letters and new sounds on a weekly basis as our students grow and develop phonetic skills.

Many of us have resisted asking our students to practice letters and sounds in isolation, however. As library media specialists and teachers, we've turned to examples of children's literature that we can use as we focus on the week's chosen letter. As we share books aloud with our students, learners see the week's letter and sounds put to use to create engaging stories. As we offer activities in conjunction with these books, we ensure that learners go beyond sight recognition of letters to understand how to apply letter-sound knowledge.

Steven A. Stahl makes this precise point in his 1992 Reading Teacher article entitled "Saying the 'P' Word: Nine Guidelines for Exemplary Phonics Instruction." Stahl writes that a person learning to play baseball needs not only to practice batting but must also know the broader application by having seen batting put to use in a baseball game! In just the same way, our students must learn their letters in a literacy-and-literature-rich environment where reading and writing are a daily part of their classroom activities.

I've structured this book to allow you to enhance and enrich a Letter of the Week approach by offering you several picture books to accompany each letter of the alphabet. I've also included a variety of engaging reading, writing, thinking, and creative activities to extend the learning of concepts in these picture books. Of course, these activities will also cement the letter-sound correspondence understanding that Letter of the Week was designed to promote.

Enjoy the literature. Enjoy the activities. Most of all, enjoy the learning with your young students!

—Toni Buzzeo

Toni Buzzeo, MA, MLIS, is a longtime educator and author. As a career library media specialist, she always seeks connections between children's literature and classroom concepts, skills, and practices. She is the author of 11 professional books for teachers and librarians as well as 16 picture books for children. To learn more about her and her work, visit her Web site at www.tonibuzzeo.com.

The Aunts Go Marching

by Maurie J. Manning. Boyds Mills Press, 2003.

This clever adaptation of the popular children's song, "The Ants Go Marching" is set in a city where a child is visiting her aunt. The aunt lives in an apartment building full of aunts who all go marching downtown one rainy day. The "little one," decked out in her yellow rain coat and hat, also brings along her drum, which adds to the reading fun as her recurrent Rat a tat-tat!/ Rat a tat-tat!/ Ba-rump, ba-rump, /ba-rump! sound follows every lively verse. In the end, a clap of thunder drives the legions of aunts and the "little one" back home again.

"The Ants Go Marching"

"The Ants Go Marching" is a popular children's song sung to the tune of the Civil War song, "When Johnny Comes Marching Home." It is perfect for young singers because of the extensive repetition in the lyrics and the counting aspect. (Note: You may want to teach your students the original song so that they can better appreciate this adaptation.) Lyrics and music for "When Johnny Comes Marching Home" are available at the National Institutes of Health, Department of Health & Human services Web site at kids.niehs.nih.gov/lyrics/johnny.htm and for "The Ants Go Marching" at kids.niehs.nih.gov/lyrics/antsgo.htm.

Once students have learned the original, go back to the lyrics of the book and sing them to the same tune.

Mathem"ANTICS"

Both the song and the book, *The Aunts Go Marching*, can become a math lesson about one hundred objects. Provide each student with 100 Cuisinare blocks or other easily manageable object. Direct them to place one of these "ants/aunts" on their desks or on the floor, and mimic them walking one by one. Now, add a second "ant/aunt" behind the first, and add a second parallel line for two by two, and so on until all 100 are in use. You might want to sing "The Ants Go Marching" as a class while doing this activity!

To extend the lesson, read another book about 100 ants:

📖 **Book Pairing:** *One Hundred Hungry Ants* by Elinor J. Pinczes, illustrated by Bonnie MacKain. Houghton Mifflin, 1993.

Again, using the same 100 Cuisinare blocks or other objects, mimic the recombinations of ants seen in the story.

Sounds the Same/Means Something Different

Manning has made delightful use of the homophones "ant" and "aunt" in rewriting the lyrics to the song. (Note: Homophones are two words that sound the same—and may be spelled the same or differently—but mean something different. Depending on the region of the country you live in, "aunt" may be pronounced "ant.")

Begin by inviting your students to define the two words "ant" and "aunt." Now ask them to brainstorm other homophones, such as ate/eight and be/bee. How many can they think of?

My Favorite Ant/Aunt

Ask students to bring in a photograph of their favorite aunt, and provide them with drawing materials. Invite them to create a portrait of that aunt. Explain that a portrait artist tries to capture the personality of the subject by focusing on his or her head, face, and expressions. Ask them to capture this person from the shoulders up. For those students who may not have a favorite aunt, offer the choice to create a portrait of their favorite ant. Other students may choose to do both!

Art

**by Patrick McDonnell.
Little, Brown and Company, 2006.**

Art (the boy) is a maker of art (the creative expression). His art is play in the same way that Harold's art is play in *Harold and the Purple Crayon*. His imagination and his markers work together to make worlds of shapes that stand alone or grow to be a whole world on their own.

Artists Make Art

Begin by asking your students what they think art is. After a discussion that expands upon students' ideas, share the definition of "art" from a good primary dictionary such as *Merriam-Webster's Primary Dictionary* by Ruth Heller (2005). If students are familiar with the use of the dictionary, ask them where they think you might find the word "art" in the dictionary to reinforce their location skills. Now ask what the word is for a person who makes art. Once you have discussed the word "artist," ask whether kids can be artists. What does the book *Art* have to say about this question?

Art and Harold

Art is a book that is quite similar to Crockett Johnson's famous book about Harold. Begin by reading that classic:

📖 **Book Pairing:** *Harold and the Purple Crayon.* Harper & Row, 1955.

Now create a Venn diagram on the board or chart paper, and ask students to compare the two stories. How are Art and Harold alike? How are they different? How is their art similar or different? How is their process similar or different?

Art inside Art

One of the hallmarks of both *Art* and *Harold and the Purple Crayon* is that both artists create on a life-size scale. Give your students this same opportunity by covering a wall in the hallway, library, or classroom with chart paper. Provide kids with markers and safety stools and instruct them to draw as close to life-size as they can. For those students who want to create pictures of objects that reach to (or are in) the sky, stand immediately behind them on a safety ladder as they draw.

Art Is a Name

Students will notice that there are two "arts" in this story (Art and art). Explain that in the English language, many names are also words (and vice versa). Give examples such as May, Jewel, Rose, Lily, Ginger, Grace, Bill, Mark, Clay, or Ridge. Once they understand the concept, ask them to try to think of some others that start with the letter A (such as Abbey, April, Angel).

If there are bilingual students in your class, you might ask them if they can think of any examples in the other language that they speak. For instance, Esperanza means hope in Spanish, and it is also a girl's name. Fleur means flower in French, and like Esperanza, it is also a girl's name.

Name that Person

Spend some time talking about why Axle Annie's name suits her job. Using a model vehicle, explain what an axle is and show how it works. Now, brainstorm a list of names that start with the letter A. If you have A names in your class begin with those. Then, pair each with an appropriate noun or adjective to create a new name. (Note: You may need to brainstorm a list of nouns and adjectives beginning with A before you launch this activity.)

Axle Annie Adventure

Share the second Axle Annie picture book with your students:

📖 **Book Pairing:** *Axle Annie and the Speed Grump* by Robin Pulver, illustrated by Ted Arnold. Dial, 2005.

Now challenge them to come up with a third Axle Annie adventure. After soliciting their ideas for the characters and plot, choose one idea and actually write the story with them. When it is complete, assign each student or pair of students to create an accompanying illustration.

Snow Day!

Regardless of the climate in your region, students will have fun imagining what they might do on a snow day from school.

Begin by sharing a few other picture books on the topic:

📖 **Book Pairing:** *Snow Day!* by Lester Laminack, illustrated by Adam Gustavson. Peachtree Publishers, 2007.

Snow Day! by Patricia Lakin, illustrated by Scott Nash. Dial, 2002.

Snow Day by Lynn Plourde, illustrated by Hideko Takahashi. Simon & Schuster, 2001.

Now, with students, create a list of all of the activities mentioned in these stories that could fill a snow day with fun. Once you have an extended list, challenge them to find as many activities as possible that begin with the letter A; for example: Make snow angels. (Note: This may require re-writing some items on your list to include a noun, verb, or adjective that begins with A. For example, if "paint a picture" is on your list, it might be changed to "make art," and "summersaults in the snow" might be changed to "acrobatics.")

Snow Day Activity Mural

After completing the Snow Day! activity above, invite your students to create a bulletin board or wall mural with a single large scene depicting the various snow day activities they listed. Label each activity with its name, emphasizing the letter A by using a larger font or another color.

Sorting Apples

Visit your local farm market or grocery store and buy one or more of each type of apple you can find (see *Apple Farmer Annie* for a list of suggested varieties). Place them all on a table in the library or classroom and invite students (with well-washed hands) to devise different sorting schemes for them (color, size, shape, etc.). After this sorting activity, wash the apples with a fruit wash and then invite students to join you in a tasting activity. Slice the apples into thin pieces and record student preferences on an Apple Preferences chart.

Appetizing Apples

From her apples, Annie creates delicious apple cider as well as applesauce, muffins, cakes, and pies. Plan an apple feast for your students. You may want to make applesauce or apple cider with them as a class, or you may decide to solicit some homemade apple baked goods from parents or the school cafeteria to round out your menu.

My Apple Recipes

Wellington includes three recipes at the back of *Apple Farmer Annie*. Create a cookbook, as pictured on the "Annie is tired but happy" page, using the My Apple Recipes templates on page 10. Solicit favorite apple recipes from parents of your students to include in the book.

Apple Counting

Using the apple template (see page 11) or your school's die-cut machine, create a stack of paper apples in various colors—red, yellow, and green as well as a pile of +, -, and = operation signs and numbers from 1 through 10. Now, invite students to create a series of mathematical equations by gluing various numbers of apples, operation signs, and numerals onto paper. (See below for example.)

My Apple Recipes

Name: _____

My Recipe: _____

Apple Template

Baby Bear's Books

by Jane Yolen, illustrated by Melissa Sweet. Harcourt, 2006.

In rhymed, first-person narrative verse, Baby Bear recounts his day of books and stories, from the first book that was read while he and his brother bounced on the bed; to his snack time read with Mama; to his cozy naptime story; to his before-, during-, and after-supper books. The day ends with a bath and one last book, read once again in his cozy bed.

When and Where?

Baby Bear loves to read—anytime, anywhere! Re-read the story and ask students to stop you each time Baby Bear asks for a book to be read aloud, or when he reads a book himself. Ask what time of day it is, and what event is happening (e.g., naptime), where Baby Bear is, and what he wants to read. Record each instance on a chart with three columns. The columns should be labeled WHEN, WHERE, and WHAT.

Reading Time

Ask students to discuss the times that they like to read. Begin with a duplicate list of all of the times Baby Bear wants to read. Go around the room and ask students to talk about their favorite reading times. Each time a student mentions a reading time that matches one of Baby Bear's, mark the student's name next to Baby Bear's time on the list. Whenever a student offers a new favorite time, add it to the bottom of the list with the student's name.

At the end of the activity, ask each student to draw a picture of the time they like to read best. Attach a sentence that reads:

My favorite time to read is

_____.

Create a class book or bulletin board display.

Favorite Books

Each time Baby Bear describes the kind of book he wants to read, ask students to try to think of a book that Baby Bear might like. To help them out, you may want spread out a large pile of books that qualify in the middle of your circle. If you do, take turns allowing students to select a book that meets Baby Bear's criteria from the pile.

At the end of the activity, invite students to explore the books in the circle.

My Book Log

Help students to create a book log in which they can write the time and place of each book they read along with the title. Ask them to decorate an oak tag book cover that is titled, MY BOOK LOG by _____. Between the front and back covers, insert several pages based on the template on page 16.

Tasting Bee-bim Bop

Following the recipe in the back of *Bee-bim Bop*, prepare this popular Korean dish with your students using an electric rice cooker and an electric wok. Allow students to take turns adding ingredients and be sure to serve the meal in a traditional manner so that all children have a chance to mix-mix!

Before and After

Read *Bee-bim Bop* several times, emphasizing the order of events. Now, create several sets of sequence cards with images and/or phrases to represent the steps in the process. Divide students into groups. Give each group a set of sequence cards and ask students to arrange them in the order of events in the book.

How Do You Spell Delicious?

Ask students to look at the name bee-bim bop, then ask how many Bs there are in that name. Invite students to brainstorm other foods that begin with the letter B. Challenging them to think of a food that has more than one word beginning with B, such as banana bread.

Once the brainstormed list is complete, challenge students to divide the listed foods into the six food groups according to the new FDA food pyramid. Use the How Do You Spell Delicious? graphic organizer (see page 17) to record their answers. (Note: For more information on the food pyramid for kids, visit ki dshealth.org/kid/stay_healthy/food/pyramid. html).

Acrostic

As a class, choose bee-bim bop or another food from the list created above in the How Do You Spell Delicious? activity to create an acrostic poem. For example:

> Bright green pods
>
> Eat them steamed
>
> And stir-fried
>
> Nothing else tastes so good

We're Going on a B Hunt

Brave Bitsy and the Bear is rich with B words, from brave, Bitsy, and Bear to beavers, bracken, and blanket. After you read the book once for enjoyment, outfit your students with We're Going on a B Hunt glasses (see template on page 18) and return to the text with all eyes tuned for B words. As you encounter each one, add them to a list on the board or chart paper.

Next, take some time to define each word. Ask students to first formulate a definition, based on personal knowledge. Then, using a primary dictionary such as *Merriam-Webster's Primary Dictionary* by Ruth Heller (2005), refine your definition.

Brave Is as Brave Does

After reading *Brave Bitsy and the Bear* aloud to your students, discuss what it means to be brave. Once you have a working definition, ask students to think about what makes Bitsy brave in this story. Next, raise the question of whether Bear is also brave. If so, what does he do that shows us his bravery?

Next, read another story about a brave character:

📖 **Book Pairing:** *Brave Irene* by William Steig. Farrar, Straus and Giroux, 1986.

Discuss the ways in which Irene shows that she is brave. In what ways is her bravery similar to Bitsy's? In what ways is it different?

Now challenge students to draw an illustration of themselves being brave and write a sentence to describe what happened. Display the drawings and sentences along with the cover of *Brave Bitsy and the Bear.*

Sleepy Bears

Poor Bear! He is so sleepy. It's nearly time for him to hibernate, but he wants to help Bitsy find her way home first. After reading the story, ask students to remember the three tricks Bitsy used to keep Bear awake on their journey.

Now, take a trip across the playground or through the hallways of the school. You play the part of Bear and ask your students to be the Bitsy rabbits. Re-enact the three times when Bitsy keeps Bear awake. (Note: You may first want to practice bouncy, wide-awake songs, marching songs, and a loud TARANTARA! cry.)

When you return to the classroom or library, have a large cutout of Bear prepared on the bulletin board or wall. Invite the students to become various woodland animals and, using scraps of construction paper, scissors, markers, and glue sticks, design and attach appropriate coverings to keep bear snuggly warm all winter as Bitsy and her woodland friends do in the story.

Let Sleeping Bears Lie

A reading of *Brave Bitsy and the Bear* is a perfect opportunity to introduce students to hibernation. After a first reading, discuss hibernation. Ask students what they know about this long winter sleep, and list their responses. After students have contributed their ideas, share several fiction and nonfiction books with them:

📖 **Book Pairing:** *Bear Dreams* by Elisha Cooper. Greenwillow Books, 2006.

Bear Snores On by Karma Wilson, illustrated by Jane Chapman. Margaret K. McElderry Books, 2002.

Every Autumn Comes the Bear by Jim Arnosky. Putnam, 1993.

Hibernation by Margaret Hall. Capstone Press, 2008.

Time to Sleep by Denise Fleming. Henry Holt, 1997.

Now, return to your hibernation fact list and add new information. You may want to correct any facts that were previously misstated. If you have additional time, write a group story about Bear's next winter hibernation and compare it to when Bitsy helped him hibernate.

Beetle Bop

by Denise Fleming. Harcourt, 2007.

In jaunty, bebopping verse, Fleming captures the wide variety of physical characteristics, behavior, and habitats of the many kinds of beetles that live all around the world. The gorgeous illustrations were created by pouring colored cotton fiber through hand-cut stencils.

Beetle Neighbor

In her end note, Fleming asks readers, "What kinds of beetles live near you?" Take your students on an exploratory journey to answer this question. Consider one or more of the following avenues:

- Visit the school library nonfiction or reference shelves to check out insect field guides and nonfiction books about beetles.

- Take a field trip to an environment likely to have several types of beetles.

- Contact a college or university near you to inquire whether there is an entomologist available to come to speak to the class (and perhaps bring samples).

Ask students to choose one local beetle to draw, color, and label. Display them with the cover of *Beetle Bop*.

Build a Beetle

According to Fleming in her end notes, "all beetles have three body segments and six legs, and almost all have two sets of wings—a front set that protects the second set, which is used for flying." Provide students with bins full of each of the three body parts (head, thorax, abdomen; see page 19), legs, and wings cut out of various types of paper (see page 20; consider cutting wings out of lighter weight paper). Invite students to construct one or more beetles and decorate them.

Beautiful Beetles

After reading *Beetle Bop*, engage your students in reading a pair of nonfiction books about beetles:

📖 **Book Pairing:** *The Beautiful Beetle Book* by Sue Unstead, illustrated by Gill Tomblin. Waterbird Books, 2005.

The Beetle Alphabet Book by Jerry Pallotta, illustrated by David Biedrzycki. Charlesbridge, 2004.

As you read, ask them to note colors, physical descriptions, and behavior/actions of the beetles described and make a list of these on chart paper or the board. When your list is complete, craft phrases that you can add to Fleming's text and illustrate them accordingly.

When the Beetles Go Marching In

(Sung to the tune of "When the Saints Go Marching In.")

Oh, when the beetles go marching in,
Oh, when the beetles go marching in,
Oh, then I'll see the June bugs and ladybugs,
Oh, when the beetles go marching in.

Oh, when the beetles begin to crawl,
Oh, when the beetles begin to crawl,
Oh, then I'll see the scarab and stag beetles,
Oh, when the beetles begin to crawl.

Oh, when the beetles come flying in,
Oh, when the beetles come flying in,
Oh, then I'll see the fireflies and lightning bugs,
Oh, when the beetles come flying in.

Oh, when the beetles begin to click,
Oh, when the beetles begin to click,
Oh, then I'll hear the click beetles and skipjacks,
Oh, when the beetles begin to click.

My Book Log Template

My Book Log

Title

_____

Time I Read This Book

_____

Place I Read This Book

_____

My Book Log

Title

_____

Time I Read This Book

_____

Place I Read This Book

_____

My Book Log

Title

_____

Time I Read This Book

_____

Place I Read This Book

_____

My Book Log

Title

_____

Time I Read This Book

_____

Place I Read This Book

_____

Grains	Vegetables	Fruits	Fats and Oils	Milk/Dairy Products	Protein (meats, fish, beans, nuts)

We're Going on B Hunt Glasses

Build a Beetle

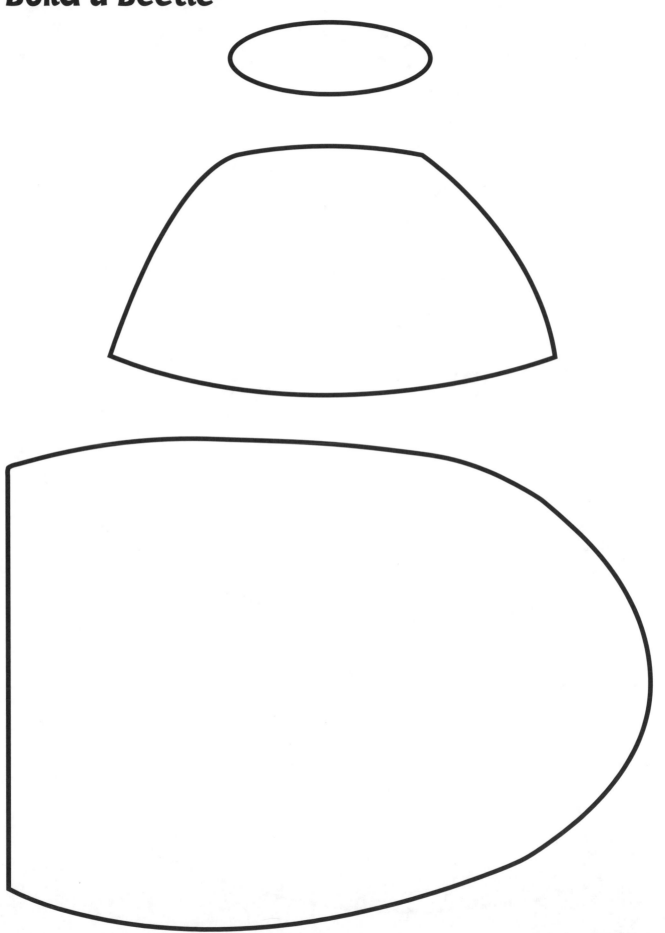

The Costume Copycat

by Maryann Macdonald, illustrated by Anne Wilsdorf. Dial, 2006.

Despite Angela's enthusiasm, it is always big sister Bernadette's Halloween costume that is the most successful. Bernadette's costume always looks great; works with the weather; and receives the most attention from Mrs. Walker, the neighbor who makes candy apples. So every Halloween, Angela chooses to wear Bernadette's costume from the previous year. But finally, Angela steals the show when she designs her own spectacularly creative ghost costume!

Costume Capers

Ask students to tell you about their most recent Halloween costume, and list the costumes on a chart. Now, ask students to use their critical thinking skills to discuss the advantages and disadvantages of each costume listed by asking these questions:

- Would this be a good costume if the weather were cold?

- Would this be a good costume if it were raining?

- Would this be a good costume if the best costume made you look beautiful/handsome?

Each time the answer is no, ask students to think of a better costume for the situation, either from the list or an original idea.

Copycats!

Begin with a discussion of the word "copycat." Ask students to tell you what they think a copycat is. Work with them to form a definition of the word and then introduce (or review) the dictionary. Read them a definition from an excellent primary level dictionary such as *Merriam-Webster's Primary Dictionary* by Ruth Heller (2005).

Then, ask them to practice copycatting. Ask two students to begin. One will be the speaker and one will be the copycat. Ask the copycat to repeat, one sentence at a time, everything the speaker says. Now, switch the copycatting to actions. A different student will be the actor and a second will be the copycat. Ask the copycat to repeat, one at a time, each action of the actor.

End with a discussion of Angela's copycatting in the book. Did it work out well for her? What worked better? Discuss the disadvantages of copycatting and the advantages of originality.

No More Costume Copycat

Ask students to imagine that they are Angela on the Halloween that she decided to make her very own costume. Instruct them to draw a picture of their imagined costume. Remind them that Angela added more and more details to her costume to make it special. Ask them to do the same.

When students have finished their drawings, post them on a No More Costume Copycat bulletin board.

"Scary Costume"

Robert Pottle is a Maine children's poet who specializes in funny poetry. Visit his Web site at www.robertpottle.com/poems/halloween-poems.php and click on the link to the poem "Scary Costume." It is short enough that you and your students will be able to memorize and perform it for other classes—and teachers!

The Cow Who Clucked

by Denise Fleming. Henry Holt, 2006.

One morning Cow awakens—and clucks! She traverses the farm, resolved to find her moo. She runs into Dog, Bee, Cat, Fish, Duck, Goat, Mouse, Snake, Squirrel, and Owl. Each time she clucks, they answer with their appropriate animal sound. Finally, as the shadows grow long, Cow shuffles past Hen. You've already guessed that she responds with a moo! The two animals trade sounds and, under a sky of moon and stars, they return to their happy mooing and clucking.

Sound-Off

When Cow's moo went to Hen, Cow acquired a sound that began with the same letter as her name. Challenge your students to think of other animal sounds that also begin with C. (You may want to introduce the concept of the Ch sound here, as well.) Examples might include caw, croak, chitter, chirp, etc.

Make a list of all of the animal sounds they think of, and next to each sound, write the name of the animals that makes it. Do any of these animals have names that also begin with C?

Extend the activity by making a list of all of the animals that Cow encountered. Ask students to think of an animal sound that begins with the same letter as each of their names, even though it may NOT be the sound that animal makes. For example, cat/crow, snake/squawk, etc.

"Old MacDonald Had a Farm'"

Consider using the results of the final Sound-Off activity above to create a scrambled version of "Old MacDonald Had a Farm":

Old MacDonald had a farm.

E-I-E-I-O

And on his farm he had a _____. (animal starting with a particular letter)

E-I-E-I-O

With a _____ _____ here (sound starting with that same letter, whether or not the animal makes that sound)

And a _____ _____ there.

Here a _____.

There a _____.

Everywhere a _____ _____.

Old MacDonald had a farm.

E-I-E-I-O

For example, you might sing, "On his farm he had a goat," and then have the goat growl!

Animal Speak

Begin this activity with the letter C and then extend it to include other letters your students have already studied this year.

In the center of the Animal Speak Graphic Organizer (page 26), place a letter. In the second ring, place the name of all of the animals students can think of that start with that letter. In the third ring, write the sound that each animal makes.

Cows for Kids

Consider introducing your students to the Cows for Kids livestock program for the children of Northern Kenya sponsored by The Boma Fund, Inc., and founded by Joseph Lekuton, an award-winning author. Visit the Cows for Kids Web site at www.cowsforkids. org to learn more about how you and your students can be involved in buying cows for nomadic families recovering from the drought in northern Kenya.

When Does a C Not Sound Like a C?

As you read *Cha-Cha Chimps*, your students are sure to notice that these words begin with C. But they are also likely to notice that they don't make the hard C sound that the C in Cat makes, but the softer, diagraph CH sound. For those who have not noticed, call their attention to it.

Now brainstorm with your students other words that begin with CH. You may want to search the text of *Cha-Cha Chimps* first, to find "cheetah" and "chicos" in the "6" verse. From there, allow students to make the CH sound and then think of a word that follows.

Create a list of these CH words. Then, to reinforce the difference, create a brainstormed list of words with the hard C initial sound.

Cha-Cha-Cha

After reading (or even while you read!) *Cha-Cha Chimps*, students will be ready to dance. Of course, you'll want to begin with the cha-cha. If you'd like clear video instructions, the University of Louisville has two cha-cha lessons posted on YouTube (the men's part and the women's part).

Men's Cha-Cha

<youtube.com/watch?v=FnfQLBhCXK4>

Women's Cha-Cha

<youtube.com/watch?v=7OAVKImoogY>

Or access an excellent series of short cha-cha videos at www.ehow.com/videos-on_3082_cha cha-dance-lessons.html.

Students will be eager to try every variety of dance in the book. Invite your physical education teacher to get involved, and work your way through them all!

Check Out Chimpanzees

The chimpanzees in *Cha-Cha Chimps* are unlike any you are likely to see in the zoo. One of the things that makes this book so much fun is that chimps are actually known for their clowning behavior, at least in the media. Lead students on a search for true information about chimpanzees by checking the library shelves for nonfiction books such as:

📖 **Book Pairing:** *Chimpanzees* by Karen Kane. Lerner Publishing Group, 2005.

Chimpanzees by Julie Murray. Abdo Publishing Group, 2002.

After taking notes on the facts you have learned about chimpanzees, create a Check Out Chimpanzees display for the classroom.

"If You'd Love to Chew Some Chocolate"

(Sung to the tune of "If You're Happy and You Know It")

If you'd love to chew some chocolate
Clap your hands.
If you'd love to chew some chocolate
Clap your hands.
If you'd love to chew some chocolate
and you really want to chow down
If you'd love to chew some chocolate
Clap your hands.

If you'd love to chew some corn chips
Stamp your feet.
If you'd love to chew some corn chips
Stamp your feet.
If you'd love to chew some corn chips
and you really want to chow down,
If you'd love to chew some corn chips
Stamp your feet.

If you'd love to chew some cheddar cheese
Nod your head.
If you'd love to chew some cheddar cheese
Nod your head.
If you'd love to chew some cheddar cheese
and you really want to chow down,
If you'd love to chew some cheddar cheese
Nod your head.

If you'd love to chew some cherries
Do all three.
If you'd love to chew some cherries
Do all three.
If you'd love to chew some cherries
and you really want to chow down,
If you'd love to chew some cherries
Do all three.

Clickety Clack

by Rob and Amy Spence, illustrated by Margaret Spengler. Viking, 1999.

A relatively quiet little train starts down the track in this cumulative tale, but as talking yaks, tumbling acrobats who sing, a quacking troupe of dancing ducks, two packs of stamping elephants, and two very sly mice board the train, the cacophony becomes too much for Driver Zach, who threatens to put the train into reverse. Thereafter, the train continues on its way with only the clickety clack of the wheels to disturb the silence.

The Sound of Wheels on a Track

Clickety clack is the sound the wheels of the little black train make as it rolls down the track. Challenge your students to imagine other vehicles that might make a clickety clack sound. Create a list of them. Ask students, in groups of two or three, to choose one of these other vehicles and create a list of five groups of riders who might be waiting to get onto that vehicle and make a lot of noise. (Note: You may encourage them to have the final group be a tiny creature with a very big noise planned, like the mice in *Clickety Clack*.)

Once each group has a vehicle with a list of five groups of riders, ask them to illustrate the vehicle fully loaded. If the class has study buddies whom they regularly work with, you may want to invite those buddies to join the groups to write a story modeled on *Clickety Clack*.

Who's Boarding that Train?

Divide the class into two teams. Challenge teams to a friendly competition. Explain that they will create a new list of animal groups that might be boarding the train in *Clickety Clack*, using the Who's Boarding the Train? graphic organizer (see page 27). Instruct them to think of animals and insects that begin with C. Award one point for each of these, but award two points if the sound that they make also begins with C. Therefore meowing cats would get one point, but cawing crows, chirping crickets, clucking chickens, or chittering chimpanzees would get two.

Who's That Typing?

One of the other familiar machines that makes a clickety clack sound is the typewriter. Many of your students will never have seen a typewriter. Therefore, when you bring one in to share with the group, be prepared for astonishment! Invite each student to take a turn typing his or her name followed by as many words beginning with C as they can think of and type in two minutes. (Note: You may want to introduce a series of short phonetic words for this activity, e.g., cab, cap, car, cat, etc.)

"I'm a Little Black Train"

(Sung to the tune of "I'm a Little Teapot")

I'm a little black train on the track.

My engine's in the front.

My caboose is in the back.

When my freight is loaded, clickety clack,

Out I'll go, and then I'll come back.

Animal Speak Graphic Organizer

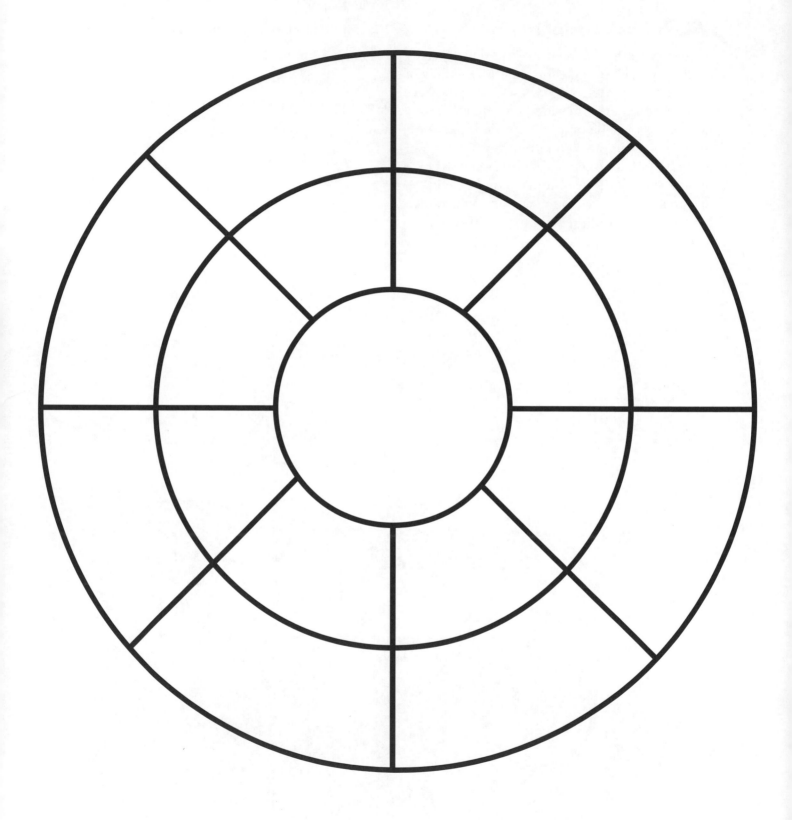

Who's Boarding the Train?

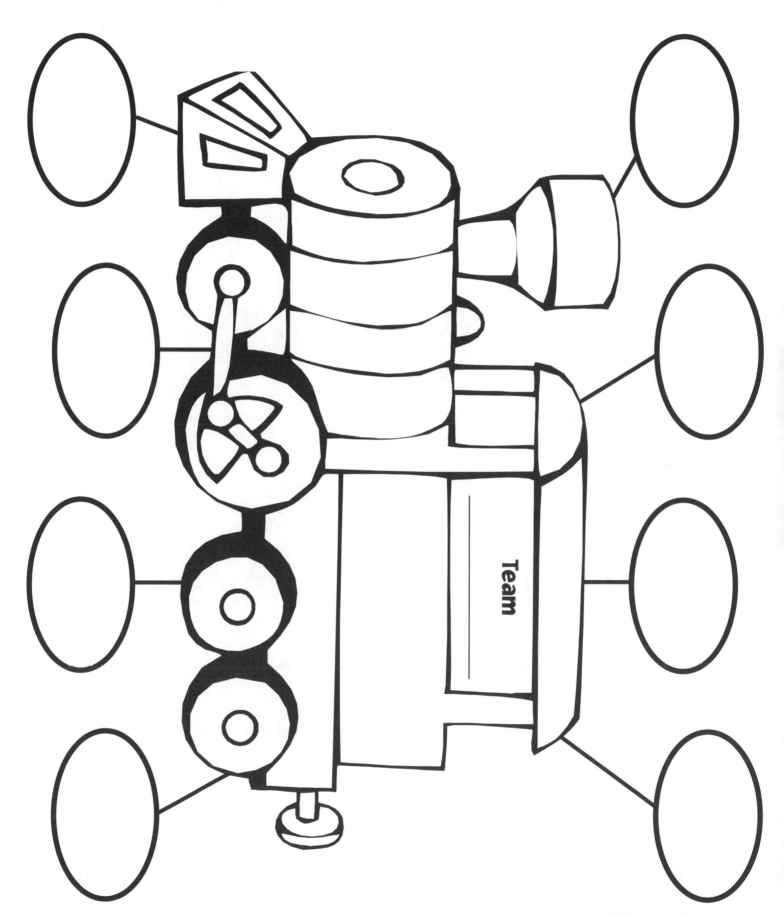

Team

Dumpster Diver

by Janet S. Wong, illustrated by David Roberts. Candlewick Press, 2007.

The neighborhood kids join Steve the Electrician, dressed in his dumpster diver duds, for weekend dives for buried treasure in the backstreet alley dumpsters. Throw-aways can become ANYTHING the kids want them to be with Steve's help and a healthy dose of imagination. In the end, when Steve is injured and is rushed to the hospital, it's the kids, with the help of the best trash finds, who create a fabulous wheelchair for his recovery.

Diving for Treasure

Ask students what it means to dive. Once they have created a good definition for the word, ask them what a diver does. There is a clue to one of the more common activities of a diver on the first page: "you can dive for treasure in the ocean." Share another book about diving, this one for ocean treasure:

📖 **Book Pairing:** *Sunken Treasure* by Gail Gibbons. HarperCollins, 1988.

Dumpster Diving

Stage a dumpster dive for the class. Fill a large plastic tub with small objects, some of which begin with D (dinosaur, dime, dish, dog, diaper). Now, one at a time, allow students to "dive" for treasure, hoping to come up with as many items that begin with D during their timed dive (try 20–30 seconds on the first round). Do not allow the remaining kids to watch each diver as that will give later students an unfair advantage in the game, whose goal is to get the most D items in a single turn. Tally the results for all to see.

Dumpster Delights

After reading *Dumpster Diver*, open a discussion with your students about why we have dumpsters. What items does Steve find in the dumpster outside his apartment? List them. Now ask students to think about all of these items. Are there better ways to handle these things than throwing them in the dumpster? Of course, Steve and his young friends think so. Ask your students to generate more recycling ideas.

Ask students to think about the things their families throw into the trash or dumpster. Are there ways that families can produce less trash? Reuse? Repair? Restore? Recycle? Discuss these concepts with the class and ask each student to draw a picture of one item that they have thrown out that could have been used in a different way, instead.

"Dumpster Diving in the Back Alleyway"

Sing this song to the tune of "Sailing, Sailing." You can find lyrics and a midi-file for the original song at the National Institutes of Health, Department of Health & Human Services Web site at kids.niehs.nih.gov/lyrics/sailing.htm.

Dumpster diving in the back alleyway

where many a treasure will be found

'ere Steve comes home again.

Dumpster diving in the back alleyway

where many a treasure will be found

'ere Steve comes home again.

Imagine a Dragon

Sophie has a huge imagination. It's so big that she imagines a dragon creeping through the cat flap downstairs into her living room as he expands in size. Ask students to imagine what Sophie's dragon might look like. Give each student a sheet of drawing paper and ask them to draw the dragon that Sophie imagines downstairs—or the one that they imagine as they listen to Sophie's story.

Dragon Fighters

Sophie dresses up three times to fight the dragon, as a knight, as a firefighter, and as a princess. Invite your students to bring in various hats and costumes in which they can dress up to fight the dragon. Once all costume elements are assembled from home contributions and the dress-up corner, stage a dragon hunt parade through the school.

Downstairs Dragons and Other Frights

Sophie imagines there is a dragon downstairs at her house. Your students may have imagined other monsters at their houses—in closets, under beds, in the attic, or in the basement. Invite them to talk about the things they fear are hidden in their houses. Ask each student to name something fearsome and talk about where the creature hides. Create a matrix like the one below to record their respective imagined creatures and their locations (add as many location columns as are necessary).

	Basement	Attic	Closet	Under the Bed
Dragon				
Two-headed monster				
Ghoul				

Dragon Poetry

Share some of the 17 dragon poems from the following book of dragon poetry with your students:

📖 **Book Pairing:** *The Dragons are Singing Tonight* by Jack Prelutsky, illustrated by Peter Sis. Greenwillow Books, 1993.

Engage students in a discussion about the narrator of each poem, the tone of the poem, and whether any of the poems is similar to the story told in *There's a Dragon Downstairs*.

If extra time is available, ask students to illustrate the poem of their choice.

Ducking into Research

I researched mallard ducks before writing Dawdle Duckling to be sure that all of the facts about the ducks in my fictional story were true. Invite your students to also conduct some duck research in the library. As you read from nonfiction books about ducks, ask students to stop you each time they hear information about how ducks look (physical appearance), where they live (habitat), what they do (behavior), and how they live together (family and young). Record this information in note form on 5x7" cards or on chart paper. When you have completed your notes, organize them into the four categories and write a short class book about ducks. Choose books from the nonfiction collection such as:

  📖 **Book Pairing:** *Duck* by Louise Spilsbury. Heinemann Library, 2005.

  Ducks by Gail Gibbons. Holiday House, 2001.

  Ducks Don't Get Wet by Augusta Goldin, illustrated by Helen K. Davie. HarperCollins, 1999.

You may also want to use a primary-level encyclopedia to gather additional information such as *Discovery Encyclopedia* (2009).

D for Doing

Introduce students to the concept of alliteration if you have not already discussed it. Then, re-read *Dawdle Duckling* and challenge students to identify the five pairs of alliterative verbs in the story (remind them that verbs are action words). Once you have written all five pairs on the board or a chart, ask students to identify the two pairs of alliterative verbs that begin with D. Then ask students to come up with additional verbs that begin with D such as "dive" and "drive."

When the verb list is complete, ask students to illustrate Dawdle Duckling doing a pair of the new activities, even if he has to leave the water to do so!

Duck Adaptations

Like all animals, ducks' bodies are specially adapted, allowing them to live successfully in their watery environment. Begin by discussing animal adaptation in general, brainstorming with students about animals they know and what their special adaptations are. Then, focus closely on duck adaptations. Ask them to think about a duck's body and its environment. What features of its body are perfectly matched to the place it lives? Read more about duck adaptations in nonfiction books from the library media center or at the Web site www.greenwing.org/teachersguide/spring99/sprs ftxt.html.

Now create a bulletin board or large chart that lists the duck body part—with student illustration—next to the function it serves.

Read the following fiction picture book to round out the activity:

  📖 **Book Pairing:** *Do Like a Duck Does* by Judy Hindley, illustrated by Ivan Bates. Candlewick Press, 2002.

"Five Little Ducks"

Sing this well-known children's song about five little ducklings who, like Dawdle, go off and get lost from their mother. You can find lyrics and a midi-file for the original song at the National Institutes of Health, Department of Health & Human Services Web site at kids.niehs.nih.gov/lyrics/fiveducks.htm.

Dinosnores

by Kelly DiPucchio, illustrated by Ponder Goembel. HarperCollins, 2005.

Millions of years ago, dinosaurs roamed a single supercontinent. According to this rollicking, rhyming picture book, it was their raucous snoring that led to the continental split and drift. The close-up illustrations of many dino favorites, in addition to rhyming text that begs to be chorused, will engage young readers from beginning to end.

Dinosaur Research

Begin dinosaur research by reading a nonfiction book about dinosaurs such as:

📖 **Book Pairing:** *Dinosaurs!* by Gail Gibbons. Holiday House, 2008.

Next, visit the dinosaur books in the nonfiction section of the library and invite students to select some books for paired or small-group research. Help them to choose a specific dinosaur and to record its diet (herbivore, carnivore, omnivore), its size (length, height, weight), and one interesting fact that is unique to their species of dinosaur.

Display student research findings with an illustration of their dinosaur on a bulletin board or gather them together into a class book.

Dino Drama

Invite each student to choose a dinosaur from *Dinosnores*. Then, have students create a mask of their dino using a paper plate threaded with elastic to hold it on. The paper plate can be colored with bright markers or crayons. Then, as you read the book aloud a second time, invite your troop of dinos to enact the book. (Note: You may want to encourage them to choose from the dinosaurs in the fourth

double-page spread so that they will know their precise dino snore sound, or you may invite them to choose more broadly, from winged lizards, sea creatures, or prehistoric bugs.)

Dinosaur Diorama

Supply each student or pair of students with an empty shoebox and ask them to create a dinosaur scene from the supercontinent they are introduced to in *Dinosnores*. Be sure that they have plenty of clay/playdough as well as construction paper, scissors, glue sticks, and markers.

Dinosaur Poetry Performance

Read several dinosaur poems to your students and challenge them to memorize the text of one of them. Excellent sources include the Tooter4Kids Web site at www.tooter4kids.com/DinosaurIndex/dinosaur_poems.htm as well as published poetry anthologies including:

📖 **Book Pairing:** *Dinosaur Poems* by John Foster, illustrated by Korky Paul. Oxford University Press, 2004.

Tyrannosaurus Was a Beast by Jack Prelutsky, illustrated by Arnold Lobel. HarperTrophy, 1992.

When each student has memorized his or her poem, host a performance of the poetry for the whole class, or add another class to the mix.

The Emperor's Egg

by Martin Jenkins, illustrated by Jane Chapman. Candlewick Press, 1999.

In the arctic, the biggest penguin in the world, a male Emperor Penguin, takes care of his egg now that his mate has waddled off to the sea to swim and eat all winter. The father stays at home without eating a single thing, keeping his egg warm under his tummy for two months until it is ready to hatch. When his chick pops out of its shell, he keeps it toasty and fed until the mother finally returns to take care of her baby, and he can set off to have his own meal.

Birds Lay Eggs

After reading *The Emperor's Egg*, students will know that emperor penguins lay eggs. Discuss whether they think that all penguins lay eggs and ask why. Once you've determined that penguins lay eggs because they are birds, ask which other birds lay eggs. Make a list of all of the birds that they know. When you've exhausted their knowledge, conduct some library research to add to the list. Whether you use nonfiction books with plenty of pictures from the collection, or project photos from a Web site such as enature.com, be sure to emphasize that all birds lay eggs. In fact, try to share pictures of as many different bird eggs as you can, and be sure to ask them about birds' eggs that they may already know about first-hand, such as chicken, robin, quail, etc.

Birds Aren't the Only Ones

Introduce the idea to your students that birds aren't the only animals to lay eggs. Solicit ideas for other animals that lay eggs. (Note: it may help to remind them of the various animal groups: mammals, birds, fish, reptiles, and amphibians.) As you discuss, you may hear them mention insects (such as ladybugs and beetles), reptiles (such as turtles and snakes), amphibians (such as frogs and salamanders), and fish (such as cod and salmon). Make sure that they learn about the two mammals that lay eggs, platypuses and spiny anteaters!

Two Emperors

Discuss the human version of an emperor with students. What does an emperor do? Many students may know this word from the fairy tale, "The Emperor's New Clothes." Share a version of this story to your students:

📖 **Book Pairing:** *The Emperor's New Clothes* by Hans Christian Andersen, illustrated by Virginia Lee Burton. Houghton Mifflin, 1977.

After sharing the book, again discuss what an emperor is. Ask why they think the emperor penguin has this name.

"Crack Goes the Egg"

Sing this song to the tune of "Pop Goes the Weasel." Ask one student to be the father penguin (with a small ball balanced on his or her feet). He or she will waddle like a penguin, balancing the ball, for the first two lines. Ask the remaining students to curl up into small egg shapes for the third line, then to CRACK out of the shells on lines four, five, and six.

All around the snow and the ice.

The Emperor warms his egg.

The chick is snuggling deep inside.

Then

CRACK! goes the egg.

Ella the Elegant Elephant

by Carmela and Steven D'Amico. Arthur A. Levine, 2004.

Shy Ella, who lives in the imaginary Elephant Islands, worries about making friends in her new home. When she finds her grandmother's elegant "good luck hat," she falls in love with it and wears it to her first day of school. Belinda Blue, the class bully, names her Ella the Elegant and sets the stage for bullying. However, when a recess ball lands on the top of the safety wall, and Belinda falls in trying to fetch it, Ella and her amazing "good luck hat" come to the rescue.

Elegant Elephant Attire

Introduce students to the word "elegant." Ask them what they think it means and discuss their ideas. Then read the definition from a primary dictionary such as *Merriam-Webster's Primary Dictionary* (2005). If students are familiar with the use of the dictionary, ask them where they think you might find the word "elegant" in the dictionary to reinforce their location skills.

Now ask students why they think Belinda named Ella "Ella the Elegant." What is it about her hat that fits the definition of "elegant"? Ask them to remember what their parents were wearing when they went out to a special restaurant, dance, or party. Now brainstorm what other clothing items students think are elegant attire and make a list of these. If time allows, ask them to draw one elegant item of clothing for a boy or girl elephant like Ella to wear.

Elegant Parade

Invite students to join you in creating an "elegant parade" through the halls of your school. Ask students to bring in a few elegant items to wear in the parade. You should also plan to ask fellow faculty members to contribute elegant items to use for the day. Goodwill or Salvation Army stores are excellent sources of elegance. (Note: For simplicity's sake, costume jewelry, gloves, and scarves are easy dress-up items.)

Everyday Elephants

Students will recognize that Ella is not like elephants in the wild. Introduce a discussion about the things that make Ella different from a wild elephant and list them. Now explore wild elephants with the class. You may want to begin by learning about the two different kinds of elephants, African and Asian (or Indian). After viewing pictures of each kind of elephant, ask students to decide which kind of elephant Ella might be. (Hint, since she lives on an island in the Indian Ocean, she's probably an Asian elephant).

Then, explore a variety of books and online sources of information about elephants to learn more. Videos and photographs are available for African elephants at the National Geographic Kids Web site at <u>kids.nationalgeographic.com/Animals/CreatureFeature/African-elephant</u>. Videos and photographs are available for Asian elephants at the ARKive Web site at <u>www.arkive.org/species/GES/mammals/Elephas_maximus</u>.

"Ella Elephant"

(Sung to the tune of "Twinkle, Twinkle, Little Star.")

Ella elephant you are

elegant and quite the star.

You saved Bella on the wall

when she chased the bright red ball.

Ella elephant you are

elegant and quite the star.

The Easter Egg Farm

by Mary Jane Auch. Holiday House, 1992.

Pauline is considered the lazy member of Mrs. Pennywort's henhouse because she does not produce an egg a day like the others. When she concentrates, she produces an odd looking egg with the pattern of whatever she might be looking at. When Mrs. Pennywort exposes Pauline to many sights, multi-colored chicks start to hatch from Pauline's beautiful eggs, spoiling the shells. Pauline's chicks are as interesting as she is and the farm comes to be known as Easter Egg Farm.

Whatever You See

Begin by brainstorming all of the things that Pauline concentrated on to produce her interesting eggs in *The Easter Egg Farm*. Once you have a comprehensive list, ask each student to choose the egg that he or she liked the best. Now challenge students to gather ideas for other items Pauline could concentrate on. Ask each student to create a list of the items they'd like to see as an egg.

Egg Collage

Distribute a stack of magazines to each table where students are sitting. Make sure that they represent a variety of topics and include a variety of pictures in the articles and advertisements. Now, invite students to choose five to ten pages each that feature interesting patterns that appeal to them. Ask students to flag their chosen pages with sticky notes. Once all pages are marked, visit the tables and remove the pages for the students. Using the Egg Template (see page 36), have students trace an egg shape on the best portion of the pattern with black marker. Then ask students to cut out their eggs and glue them to the Egg Collage graphic organizer surrounding the barn (see page 37).

Design an Egg

Invite students to pretend they are Pauline. Ask them to concentrate on a single object until they feel an egg coming on. Then, using a blank egg you have cut out of oaktag (use the Egg Template on page 36), they will re-create the design they are concentrating on. Create a bulletin board of the class's eggs.

"Five Little Easter Eggs"

Teach students to recite the "Five Little Easter Eggs" fingerplay. For each couplet, hold up the appropriate number of fingers on the first line. On the second line, throw hands wide and then bring them back in again, displaying the new number of fingers up. End with thumb and forefinger together for the zero sign.

"Five Little Easter Eggs"

Five little Easter eggs, scattered on the floor.
Out popped a blue chick. Then there were four.

Four little Easter eggs, lovely as can be.
Out popped a red chick. Then there were three.

Three little Easter eggs, all of them brand new.
Out popped an orange chick. Then there were two.

Two little Easter eggs, very nearly done.
Out popped a green chick. Then there was one.
One little Easter egg, alone in the sun.
Out popped a yellow chick. Then there were none.

> ## Edwina the Dinosaur Who Didn't Know She Was Extinct
>
> ### by Mo Willems. Hyperion, 2006.
>
> Everyone in town knows Edwina, who plays with the kids, does favors, and even bakes chocolate chip cookies for everyone. They all love her—except Reginald Von Hoobie-Doobie, who knows everything about just about everything, including the fact that dinosaurs are EXTINCT. He sets out to prove that dinosaurs really are extinct—even to Edwina herself. However, as convinced as Edwina is that she is extinct, she decides not to care. Nor does Reginald.

What Is Extinct?

Open a discussion with students about what it means to be extinct. Ask for their speculative definitions and then read the definition from a primary dictionary such as *Merriam-Webster's Primary Dictionary* (2005). If students are familiar with the use of the dictionary, ask them where they think you might find the word "extinct" in the dictionary to reinforce their location skills.

Once students understand that animals that are extinct no longer exist on earth, brainstorm other animals they may have heard of that are extinct. Continue this discussion by reading a book about other extinct animals:

  📖 **Book Pairing:** *The Extinct Alphabet Book* by Jerry Pallotta, illustrated by Ralph Masiello. Charlesbridge, 1993.

What Happened to the Dinosaurs?

Once your students understand extinction, explore the reasons for dinosaur extinction with them. There are many theories about the demise of these reptiles, and it will be useful to explore several different theories with the class to open up their minds to the possibilities. For help, visit the Dinosaur Floor of the Classroom of the Future™ Web site at Wheeling Jesuit University at www.cotf.edu/ete/modules/msese/dinosaur.html.

You may also want to share a book on the topic:

  📖 **Book Pairing:** *What Happened to the Dinosaurs?* by Franklyn M. Branley, illustrated by Marc Simont. HarperTrophy, 2000.

Endangered Is Not Extinct

Discuss the differences between endangerment and extinction. Since young children are likely to be nervous about the concept of animals gone forever, they may be more accepting of endangerment, where there is still hope of saving the animals.

Begin by sharing a book about endangerment:

  📖 **Book Pairing:** *Gone Wild* by David McLimans. Walker & Co., 2006.

Continue the conversation by asking students to explore pictures of various endangered animals in nonfiction books in the library.

Ask each student to choose their favorite endangered animal and draw it. Help each student to find out what that animal needs in order to be saved and write a sentence to accompany the labeled picture of the endangered animal. Create a hallway bulletin board display about endangered animals from these pictures and sentences.

Dino Poems

Share a feast of dinosaur poems with your students from the CanTeach Web site at www.canteach.ca/elementary/songspoems67.html. After you have read several dinosaur poems from the page, consider writing your own class dinosaur poem, focusing on Edwina, extinction, or some other dino topic.

Egg Template

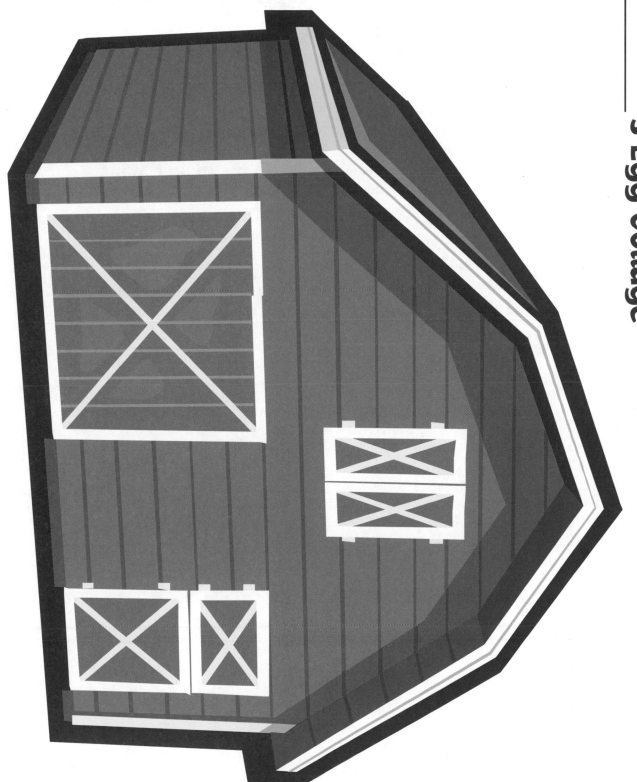

Fran's Friend

by Lisa Bruce, illustrated by Rosalind Beardshaw. Bloomsbury Publishing, 2003.

Fran's dog friend, Fred, wants to play, but Fran is busy working on a craft project. Fred tries unsuccessfully to help out by retrieving items for her that she does not need. However, when he gives up in despair, he learns that the card Fran has been making is for him.

Friendly F Names

The main characters in *Fran's Friend* both have names that begin with F: Fran and Fred. To begin this activity, create a large Venn diagram. Label one circle "Usually People Names." Label one circle "Usually Dog Names." Label the intersection "Names for Both." Now, ask students to brainstorm names of people and pets they know that begin with F. List them on the side of your chart. Next, ask students to brainstorm other F names for people and pets that they may have heard, or that they think would be a good fit. Add these to the list. Finally, place the names on the Venn diagram. Of course, there are no absolutely correct answers, but you might point out to students that a person is quite unlikely to be named Fido, while a person MAY be nicknamed Freckles (and a dog may be named Freckles too).

A Fine Friend

Fran's Friend raises the question of what makes a good friend. Reread the book and ask students to notice clues about what makes Fran a good friend to Fred. What makes Fred a good friend to Fran? Now ask each student to think of a very good friend. Ask them to name three things the person says or does that makes him or her a fine friend. Jot down the list of ideas. Then point out and discuss the qualities that are mentioned most frequently. Ask students why they think these characteristics occur repeatedly.

Going on an F Hunt

Lisa Bruce, the author of *Fran's Friend*, didn't just title her book and name her characters using the letter F. She also sprinkled the letter F all over the book by including lots of F vocabulary. Reread the story and look for all of the words that begin with F. As you find them, list them on the board and have students copy the list on circles of paper.

Now, invite students to locate and cut out pictures from a stack of expendable magazines. All of the pictures they cut out should begin with F. Ask them to create a collage of F pictures, and then glue down the F vocabulary from the book as well. Invite students to write down the new F vocabulary words related to the pictures they add to the collage.

"We Are Best Friends"

Teach students the "We Are Best Friends" song, sung to the tune of "Frère Jacques."

We are best friends.

We are best friends.

You and I.

You and I.

We can work together.

We can play together.

All day long.

All day long.

Once your students know the words, invite them to modify the fifth and sixth lines. For instance, you might replace "We can work together. We can play together" with "We can sing together. We can draw together." (Note: as you make replacements, alter the final refrain, if needed, to appropriately modify lines five and six). Sing again with their new additions.

Fortune Cookie Fortunes

by Grace Lin. Knopf, 2004.

A young narrator who thinks that the best part about eating at a Chinese restaurant is the fortune cookies introduces us to her family's five fortunes that are served up after dinner. As the story unfolds, she checks in to see whether each family member's fortune has come true. From her perspective, each fortune comes true in the lives of her family members, from contagious moods, to successful gardens, to origami-filled rooms, to well-populated bird feeders, to her own new world view.

Fortunate Fortunes

Ask students what they think a fortune is. Have they ever eaten a fortune cookie and found a fortune inside? Have they ever had a fortune teller tell their fortune? What do they know about fortunes from these experiences? Are they good news or bad news?

Now, create a tally chart on your easel with two columns. Label one column GOOD NEWS and the other BAD NEWS. As you re-read the story, ask students to listen to the fortunes. Whenever you read one, ask them to decide which column should get a mark for that fortune. At the end, ask them what conclusions they can draw about fortunes.

Write Your Own Fortunes

Part of the fun of reading Grace Lin's book is the opportunity to create fortunes for yourself and others. Because your students are young, you will want older learning buddies or plenty of adult volunteers on hand for this activity.

Ask students to think about things they would consider to be good luck. Then, direct them to team up with the volunteer "scribe" assigned to them and dictate their ideas to the scribe. The scribes will write out the fortunes on small, uniform strips of paper. Remind students that fortunes are usually 4–10 words long.

To create the "cookies" to hold these fortunes, you have two options. Either use brown construction paper circles, folded in half, glued partway around the edges and pinched in the middle (see diagram on page 42), or download and follow the clever instructions for felt "cookies" at Grace Lin's site at www.gracelin.com/content.php?page=book_fortunc&display=activities.

Have students share their fortune cookies with other students in the class or at home with their families.

Tell My Fortune

Before this activity, host a discussion with students about fortune tellers. They may be familiar with them from books, cartoons, or movies. Suggest that there might be a fortune teller coming to school soon.

Dress as a fortune teller and using a fortune ball (printable pattern available at the Family Fun Web site at familyfun.go.com/Resources/global/printables/crafts/0705_hp_fortune-teller.pdf) and allow each student to ask you a question or two.

Fortune Cookie Feast

Visit your local Chinese restaurant to purchase a bag of fortune cookies, or order them online. Create a bulletin board with a central fortune cookie that has a book-related fortune, such as "You will read many good books."

Then, host a fortune cookie feast for your students. After each student has had a chance to share his or her fortunes aloud, add the fortunes to the bulletin board.

Little Bunny Foo Foo: Told and Sung by the Good Fairy

by Paul Brett Johnson. Scholastic, 2004.

The good fairy is feeling fairly cranky. Good fairies do not like the type of tomfoolery that Little Bunny Foo Foo is likely to engage in when he takes off into the forest with a wagonload of yucky-mucky mud pies. After Foo Foo bops the field mice on their little heads with his mud pies, the Good Fairy lectures and warns him. Nevertheless, Foo Foo proceeds from field mice to woodchucks, to foxes, to grizzly bears, exhausting his chances to remain in the good fairy's good graces!

"Little Bunny Foo Foo"

Enlist students to join you in song as you turn to the lyrics and music published in the back of *Little Bunny Foo Foo: Told and Sung by the Good Fairy.* You can increase the fun by dividing the group in two, with one group singing the musical narration, and one group speaking the good fairy's part. Don't forget the fun of hand motions that can accompany the song:

"Hoppin' through the forest"—Make bunny ears with hand and hop three times.

"Scoopin'"—Make a scooping action with the left hand.

"Boppin' 'em on the head"—Bounce closed right fist on top of closed left fist.

"I don't wanna see you"—Point finger three times as if to scold.

Who's Bopping Who?

Ask the class to list the animals that Foo Foo bops on the head, one at a time. Students may notice that the animals in the book go from smallest to largest. Ask students to start with field mice once again, but this time progressing through a different series of animals, making each one larger than the last. Remind them that Foo Foo is in the forest, so all animals must be forest animals. After you've accomplished one revision, you may want to change the location to another habitat, such as the arctic. (Foo Foo could be an arctic hare!)

Good Fairies All Around

Although in traditional literature, fairies are often evil creatures, there are many instances of good fairies in children's literature. Ask students to discuss what they think a fairy is. Then share a definition of the word "fairy" from a primary dictionary such as *Merriam-Webster's Primary Dictionary* (2005). If students are familiar with the use of the dictionary, reinforce their location skills by asking them where they think you might find the word "fairy" in the dictionary.

Now ask students to think of other good fairies in books. They may mention *Cinderella, Sleeping Beauty,* or *Pinocchio,* among others. Compare the actions of those good fairies with the good fairy in *Little Bunny Foo Foo: Told and Sung by the Good Fairy.* How are they the same and different?

"Fairy Song"

Louisa May Alcott wrote a beautiful poem called "Fairy Song." You will find it on the PoetryArchive Web site at www.poetry-archive.com/a/fairy_song.html. Share the poem in full with your students. Then, depending on the developmental level of the class, you may want to teach them to memorize the first full stanza by starting each class period with the poem.

Mouse's First Fall

by Lauren Thompson, illustrated by Buket Erdogan. Simon & Schuster, 2000.

One fall day, Mouse and Minka discover red, yellow, and orange leaves tumbling and twirling all around them in a variety of shapes. They race and skip through the leaves. They pile them high, jump right in, and roll around. Finally, Mouse and Minka play hide and seek among the brightly-colored leaves, the end to a perfect fall day.

Seasons Change

Talk with students about the names of the four seasons: winter, spring, summer, and autumn. Note that in *Mouse's First Fall*, the season of autumn is called "fall." Ask them to talk about why they think that might be true. What evidence can they find in the book?

After they've discussed leaves falling, ask what else happens in nature in the fall. Make a list of the autumnal seasonal changes.

Colorful Leaves

Cut a four-inch square of clear contact paper for each student. If you have a die-cut machine, use it to cut many colors and shapes of small autumn leaves from brown, orange, red, and yellow construction paper. If you do not, use the templates on page 43 to cut out small leaf shapes and large mice and small mice (Mouse and Minka).

Place each student's contact paper square on a table with backing side up. Tape the square down to the table with rolled masking tape. Then, peel away the backing. Now invite students, one at a time, to apply a "pile" of leaves to the contact paper. Instruct them also to hide Mouse and Minka in the leaves. When each student is finished, adhere a second four-inch square of clear contact paper on top of the first, capturing the scene that the student has created. If desired, punch two holes three inches apart along the top edge, and thread yarn through. To make this a sun catcher project, use leaves cut out of fall-colored tissue paper.

A Wreath of Fall Leaves

If it is actually autumn in your town, take a walk around the school yard with the class to collect autumn leaves. If not, use the die cut machine or the leaf templates on page 43 to create leaves of a variety of colors.

Supply each child with a small luncheon-size paper plate with the center cut out. Instruct them to glue leaves all around the perimeter to create a fall leaf wreath. If you have acorns available, allow students to add these as additional decoration. After the wreaths are dry, punch a hole through the top of each and thread a piece of thick yarn through for hanging.

"The Leaves are Falling Down"

(Sung to the tune of "The Farmer in the Dell.")

The leaves are falling down.
They're yellow, red, and brown,
Hi-ho the derry-o,
The leaves are falling down.

The leaves are piling up.
Along with acorn cups.
Hi-ho the derry-o,
The leaves are piling up.

We all play hide and seek.
You're not allowed to peek.
Hi-ho the derry-o,
We all play hide and seek.

It's autumn in our town.
The leaves are falling down.
Hi-ho the derry-o,
It's autumn in our town.

Write Your Own Fortunes

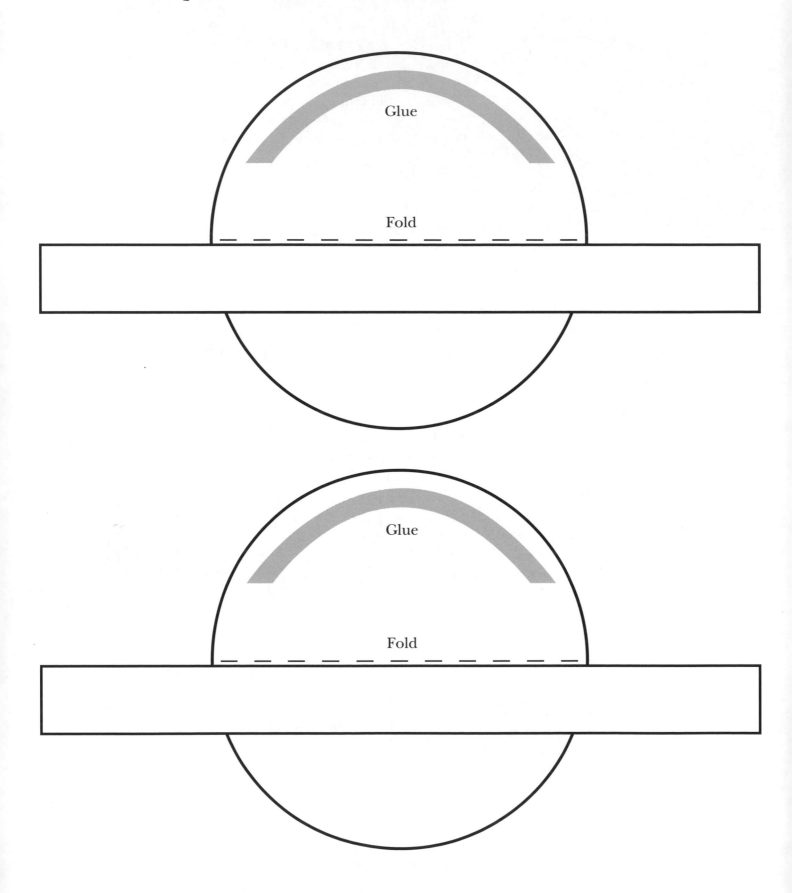

Mice and Colorful Leaves

First the Goat Ate the Shirts

Bill Grogan's Goat is a perfect story for sequencing activities because things happen in a clear progression. Create a set of story event strips with a picture of a goat to begin each statement, and a drawing of each event along with the words if you have pre-readers in your group:

Eats three shirts (x2)

Coughs up the shirts

Flags the train

Boards the train

Lands on a sheep

Gives the sheep a shirt

Sits on a pig

Gives the pig a shirt

Steps on a cow

Gives the cow a shirt

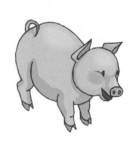

Watches the sheep, cow, and pig make a mess at the table

Using a sentence strip pocket chart, ask students to sequence the events of the story as a group, or produce multiple sets of strips and conduct this as a table activity.

Sing an Echo Song

Hoberman provides the musical score for *Bill Grogan's Goat* on the front endpapers. If you play an instrument or can entice your music teacher to do so, play the tune for students.

Bill Grogan's Goat

adapted by Mary Ann Hoberman, illustrated by Nadine Bernard Westcott. Megan Tingley Books, 2002.

As in the original children's song, when Bill Grogan's goat eats three shirts off the line, Bill, in his fury, ties the goat to the railroad track. The clever goat coughs up the three shirts at the last minute, however, and uses them to flag down the train. Hoberman extends the song by putting three other barnyard animals aboard the train who receive the shirts from the goat. The story culminates in a satisfying circle when the three shirts are once again on a line . . . and the goat once again consumes them!

Breakfast, Lunch, and Dinner with Goats

Students may or may not have encountered the myth that goats will eat anything. Since this is important background knowledge for the enjoyment of *Bill Grogan's Goat*, you will want to discuss goat eating behavior with the class before reading the story. Goats will eat plants of almost any kind, though they don't usually consume garbage, tin cans, or clothes. However, because they sometimes eat items made mostly of plant material, such as wood, they have gotten a reputation as animal garbage disposals.

After reading the story, you might also want to share another story about what a goat eats:

📖 **Book Pairing:** *Gregory the Terrible Eater* by Mitchell Sharmat, illustrated by Jose and Ariane Dewey. Simon & Schuster, 1984.

(Note: If you don't have an instrument available, you can simply sing the tune, or refer to the Kididdles Web site for the music at www.kididdles.com/lyrics/b007.html.)

Next, introduce the idea of an echo song: a song in which each line of the lyrics is sung once by a lead singer and then echoed by the group.

Sing all of the verses of the song through as they are presented in the book.

All Aboard!

Ask students to imagine what other farm animals Bill Grogan's goat might have encountered on the train. Make a list of other farm animals they know. Compare the size of these animals to a goat by labeling each animal bigger, smaller, or the same in size.

Now ask students to think about how Bill Grogan's goat made the sheep mad by landing on him, the pig mad by sitting on him, and the cow mad by stepping on him. What might Bill Grogan's goat do to make the class's list of farm animals mad?

Grumpy Gloria

by Anna Dewdney. Viking, 2006.

Gloria the bulldog feels left out, lonely, and downright GRUMPY when the youngest of three (human) siblings gets a brand-new doll for her birthday. The older siblings try everything to cheer Gloria up, offering her everything from a doggie chewy, to a brushing, a group jog, a bath, a toy, a game, and a catastrophic bike ride. Nothing works until Gloria figures out that she can insinuate herself into the doll carriage with the new doll. She doesn't need to be the one-and-only so long as she's included!

What Does It Mean?

Invite students to discuss the meaning of the word "grumpy." List all of their definitions on a chart. Next, read the definition of the word "grumpy" aloud from a primary dictionary such as *Merriam-Webster's Primary Dictionary* (2005). If students are familiar with the use of the dictionary, ask them where they think you might find the word "grumpy" in the dictionary to reinforce their location skills.

Grumpy by Any Other Name

Introduce students to the concept of synonyms, or review it if students are already familiar. Talk about how *Grumpy Gloria* author Anna Dewdney uses synonyms to avoid using the word "grumpy" too many times in the story. Reread the story aloud, and substitute "grouchy" for every synonym. Ask students whether the story is better or worse with this substitution. Why?

Then reread the story aloud and invite students to make a list of all of the synonyms for "grumpy" that they encounter. Put a star next to any words that also start with G.

Great G Names

The name of the main character in this book is Gloria. None of the human characters is named, however. Since the focus here is on the letter G, invite students to create a long list of all of the G names they know for boys, girls—and dolls. From the names you have listed, ask students to vote on a favorite name for the big brother, the big sister, the little sister, and the doll.

The Way Things Used to Be

The end papers of *Grumpy Gloria* extend the story by showing readers the sorts of things that Gloria and her youngest owner used to do (before the doll) and now do (since the doll).

Ask students to make a list of the things that the pair used to do and how they have changed now that the doll is involved. Then, direct students to create a series of statements that follow this pattern:

GLORIA and the GIRL used to _____

_____,

but now they _____

_____,

and the doll _____

_____ .

How Groundhog's Garden Grew

by Lynne Cherry. Blue Sky Press, 2003.

Squirrel catches Little Groundhog munching on his neighbor's scrumptious vegetable garden, gives Little Groundhog a scolding, and suggests he plant his own vegetables. Because Little Groundhog doesn't know how, Squirrel teaches him to harvest seeds and set aside root crops before hibernating. When spring arrives, they dig rows, plant crops, thin seedlings, transplant perennials, and water. At harvest time, Little Groundhog hosts a Thanksgiving banquet to share the fruits of his labor.

How Does a Garden Grow?

As you read *How Groundhog's Garden Grew* a second time, ask students to stop you each time that they find a step in garden growing. Write each step down on a sentence strip. When you have a full set of sentence strips representing all of the steps in creating a garden, mix them up and, using a sentence strip pocket chart, ask students to sequence the steps in creating a garden.

From Start to Finish

Ask each student to choose a favorite vegetable and write its name on the From Start to Finish graphic organizer on page 48. Using the frame illustrations in *How Groundhog's Garden Grew* or another resource, such as a seed catalog, find the seed or portion of the root needed to grow the vegetable. Ask the student to draw this in the first frame. Then, in frame two, ask

students to draw a picture of the fully grown vegetable. Finally, in frame three, ask them to draw a picture of the vegetable as it looks when it is served on the dinner table.

Grow It!

Invite students to do a little gardening of their own. Provide peat pots or paper cups of soil to each student along with fast-growing lettuce or radish seeds. Help them to plant and water their seeds, and set them on a sunny window sill.

If you feel more adventurous, you might introduce soilless gardening through hydroponics or growing sprouts. For much more information about gardening with children, visit the kidsgardening Web site at www.kidsgardening. com.

"The Garden Song"

One of the most popular gardening songs is one that children will enjoy: "The Garden Song" by Dave Mallett. Find the words to the song and a midi-file at the KidzSing Garden of Song Web site at www.gardenofsong.com/gardensng.html. Share the song with your students and send home the words so that they can teach it to their families.

Hogish Groundhogs

Groundhogs are well known for decimating gardens by munching their way through a variety of vegetables, and even flowers. Discuss the groundhog's reputation and behavior with your students. You may want to share another groundhog book with them, and then talk about why groundhogs eat food from other people's gardens, and whether or not this is good behavior.

📖 **Book Pairing:** *Groundhog at Evergreen Road* (Smithsonian's Backyard series) by Susan Korman, illustrated by Higgins Bond. Soundprints, 2003.

On the other hand, if you would like to celebrate groundhogs a bit, you can find a groundhog hat pattern at Danielle's Place of Crafts and Activities online at www.daniellesplace. com/images/groundhoghatpat.gif.

Gator Gumbo

by Candace Fleming, illustrated by Sally Anne Lambert. Farrar, Straus and Giroux, 2004.

Poor Monsieur Gator is old and gray and moving so slowly that he can no longer capture possum, otter, or skunk. Those three spry creatures taunt old Monsieur Gator until he determines to make a pot of gumbo. In the tradition of the Little Ren Hen tale, Gator invites the other animals to help and they refuse until it's time to taste that gumbo. The sly Monsieur Gator is equally willing to accommodate their greed as they slurp, slip, and plop right into the pot, just like Maman's recipe calls for.

Gators Galore

Often, alligators are both scary and exciting to kids. But in *Gator Gumbo*, it is the soft, furry animals that taunt the downtrodden old alligator—to the point that we root for the reptile! And Monsieur Gator does manage to win in the end.

To familiarize students with real 'gators living in the wild, share pictures of them with your students using an electronic white board or a data projector connected to a computer. You will find an excellent alligator photo gallery at the Florida Museum of Natural History Web site at www.flmnh.ufl.edu/herpetology/CROCS/alligatorphotos.htm, and another at the National Geographic Alligators and Crocodiles Photo Gallery at animals.national geographic.com/animals/photos/alligators-and-crocodiles/american-alligator_image.html.

Gator Gumbo in Action

Share several readings of the story to familiarize students with the story sequence and repeating dialogue. Then, using the patterns on page 49–53, create a set of stick puppets to retell the story of *Gator Gumbo*. Allow students to take turns playing the various parts until each student has had a turn.

A Gallon of Gumbo

If you have the option to cook in your library or classroom, make a pot of gator gumbo for students to enjoy. Use a slow cooker to assemble all ingredients during a morning session. (You will find a selection of recipes at the cdkitchen Web site at crockpot.cdkitchen.com/recipes/cat/1087/0.shtml). Be sure to prop a plush possum, otter, and skunk on or near the pot. Before the end of the day, remove the plush animals and serve up a small insulated paper cup to each student as you re-read *Gator Gumbo*. Ask students to decide whether they think the three rascals have fallen in.

Read-Alikes

Students who are familiar with the story of *The Little Red Hen* will recognize similarities between that story and *Gator Gumbo*. Read a version of *The Little Red Hen* aloud to students asking them to be on the lookout for things that are the same in the two stories.

📖 **Book Pairing:** *The Little Red Hen* by Jerry Pinkney. Dial, 2006.

Then, complete a Venn diagram on chart paper to compare the similarities and differences between the two stories. Once students have identified plot differences, lead them into a discussion about the differing morals of the two stories.

From Start to Finish

Name of Vegetable	

Monsieur Gator

Mademoiselle Possum

Monsieur Otter

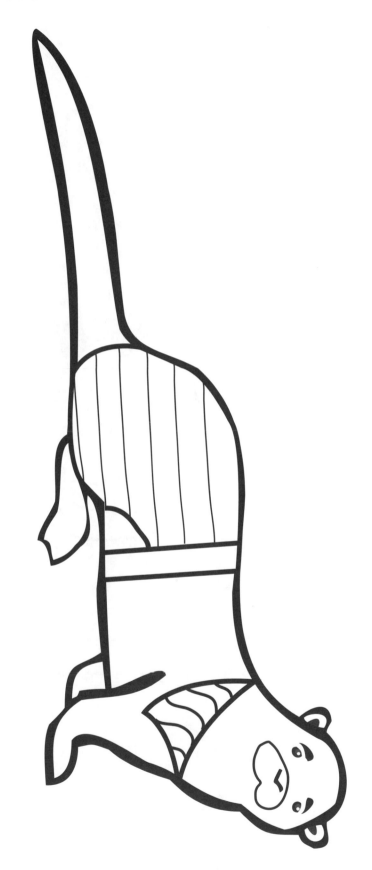

Madame Skunk

Great Big Cooking Pot

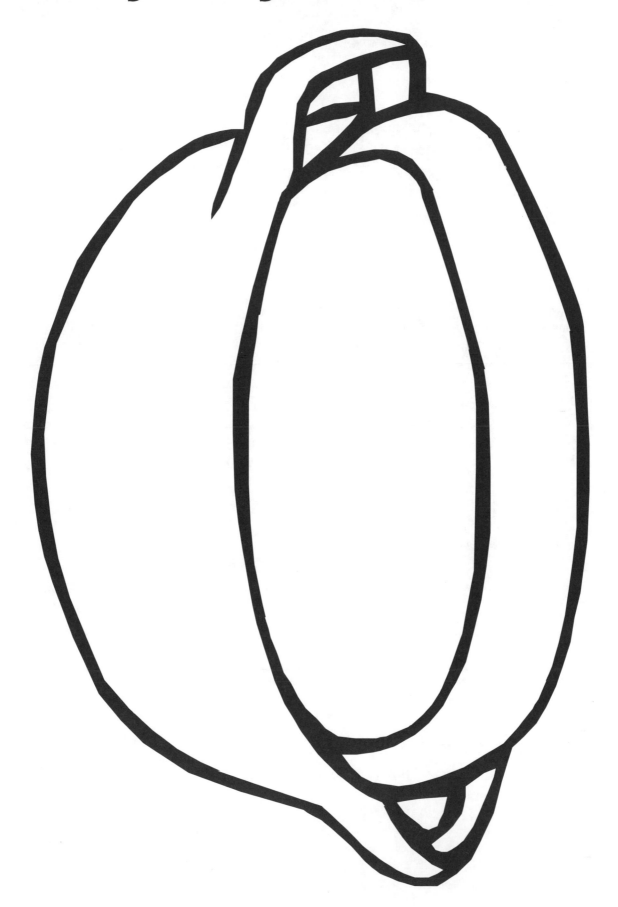

Hattie Hippo

by Christine Loomis, illustrated by Robert Neubecker. Orchard Books, 2006.

In four rhyming chapters, Hattie, a cheerful, exuberant hippo, doesn't admit to any size or ability limitations—sometimes with disastrous results. In "The Ballet," Hattie pirouettes, whirls, and twirls before leaping up high, and landing flat. "The Tea Party" would have been a wonderful event if only Hattie hadn't gotten so carried away and consumed all of the treats. In "The Swimming Pool," Hattie's cannonball proves a mistake. In "Hide and Seek," Hattie hides from Mama and falls fast asleep under the table.

Hip, Hip, Hippo

Discuss the differences between Hattie Hippo and hippos in the wild. Begin by reading a primary-level nonfiction book about hippopotami with your students such as:

📖 **Book Pairing:** *Hippopotamus* by Patricia Whitehouse. Heinemann Library, 2003.

Then, create a large Venn diagram on chart paper. Enter the factual information about hippos in the wild in one circle. Next, re-read *Hattie Hippo* and enter a list of facts about Hattie in the other circle. Are there any intersections?

Hippo Hide and Seek

Ask students to create a Hattie Hippo figure of their own on card stock using the template on page 58. Invite them to dress her and give her any accessories they'd like. Next, ask students to cut Hattie out. Then, hide one of the students' Hatties and stage a hide-and-seek game to find her. Repeat the game as time allows.

Hippo Helpers

Initiate a discussion with students about symbiosis in animals. To review the concept for yourself, read the *National Geographic* article "Odd Couples" available on the Web at magma. nationalgeographic.com/ngexplorer/0601/ articles/mainarticle.html. Explain that symbiosis is a way for animals to help each other. You may also want to read a picture book about symbiosis such as:

📖 **Book Pairing:** *Bill and Pete* by Tomie de Paola. Putnam, 1978.

Then consider sharing the National Geographic Kids video about carp hippo helpers available at the Creature Feature Web site at kids.nationalgeographic.com/Animals/ CreatureFeature/Hippopotamus. (Note: Be sure to preview the video to determine suitability for your class.)

"I Want a Hippopotamus for Christmas"

If the religious make-up of the class allows, your students will enjoy the humorous 1953 song, "I Want a Hippopotamus for Christmas." You can find lyrics and a midi-file at the National Institutes of Health, Department of Health & Human Services Web site at kids. niehs.nih.gov/lyrics/hippo.htm.

Honey . . . Honey . . . Lion! A Story from Africa

by Jan Brett. Putnam, 2005.

Honeyguide and Badger have always been partners in their pursuit of honey, but now Badger will not share, no matter how Honeyguide scolds, fusses, and fumes. Honeyguide must resort to a plan to teach him a lesson. In the morning, Honeyguide leads him over, around, and through every obstacle of the savannah, requiring him to run, swim, bound, jump, hurry, huff and puff—all the way into the lion's den—teaching all of the animals of the savannah a valuable lesson.

Hunting for H Animals

When you read the story aloud for a second time, ask students to be on the lookout for animals whose names begin with H. (Of course, they will hear the honeyguide and the honey badger mentioned on the first page, but will they hear you say guinea hens? Will they notice the hippo or the hyena in the sidebar illustrations?) Tell them they may need their detective hats to find all five H animals in the story!

A Chain of African Animals

All of the animals on the savannah get involved in Honeyguide's plan to teach the honey badger a lesson. In the end, they are all seen following Badger, rushing away from the ferocious lion and his fearsome roar. Visit Jan Brett's Web site to create a set of the animal cutouts attached to craft sticks www.janbrett. com/activities_pages_artwork.htm. Pass the cutouts around to various students. Now, as you re-read *Honey . . . Honey . . . Lion! A Story from Africa*, ask students to stand up when their animal appears in text OR illustration. Ask the remaining students to clap whenever an animal that begins with H stands up.

Who Makes Honey?

In *Honey . . . Honey . . . Lion! A Story from Africa*, the honeyguide "follows a bee to its hive, and then she leads the honey badger there to break it open with its big strong claws. Together they share the sweetness." Ask your students how many know who makes honey. Take some time to talk about how bees make honey, sharing a nonfiction book about the process:

📖 **Book Pairing:** *The Honey Makers* by Gail Gibbons. HarperCollins, 1997.

Honey Tasting

Ask students how many have tasted honey. While most may have, they may not realize that honey tastes different depending on the flowers the bees have visited. Bring this point to life by hosting a honey tasting with several kinds of honey. If your selections are limited in your local grocery, you may want to visit the Honey Locator Web site at www.honeylocator.com to find producers near you.

Set your labeled honey varieties out in shallow bowls accompanied by small tasting spoons or popsicle sticks for each variety. Instruct students that each spoon/stick may only be dipped once in order to avoid sharing germs. Discuss the flavor of each variety as you go.

You may want to chart students' favorite varieties on a large matrix. Allow each student to cast his or her vote by gluing up a tiny bee cutout (with a glue dot on the back) beneath the honey variety he/she liked best.

Tiny Bee Cutout

Horace the Horrible: A Knight Meets His Match

**by Jackie French Koller, illustrated by Jackie Urbanovic.
Marshall Cavendish, 2003.**

When the king comes down with the flu, he sends his daughter to stay at her uncle's castle, but Princess Minuette thinks cranky Sir Horace the Horrible may be aptly named. Her uncle spends his days slaying dragons and vanquishing armies, ordering Minuette to accompany him. She is unimpressed with his efforts, however, and she searches for a way to overcome her personal loneliness for her daddy. In the end, Minuette gets the hug she so desperately needs.

Horrible Is as Horrible Does (and Looks)

Begin by asking students to define the word "horrible." When discussion dies down, read the definition from a primary dictionary such as *Merriam-Webster's Primary Dictionary* (2005). If students are familiar with the use of the dictionary, ask them where they think you might find the word "horrible" in the dictionary to reinforce their location skills.

Now, ask students to think back on *Horace the Horrible: A Knight Meets His Match* and list the things that make Horace horrible. How does he look? How does he behave? Is he actually horrible inside or is it a false front, like his armor? How do they know? Ask them to support their claims with details from the text.

A Knight by Any Other Name

By the end of *Horace the Horrible: A Knight Meets His Match*, Sir Horace isn't nearly so horrible. In fact, he may have to change the sign on his door that says "Sir Horace the Horrible." Challenge your students to come up with other H words that might fill in the blank on Horace's door sign: Sir Horace the _____ _____.

Horrible or Helpful?

Give students large pieces of drawing paper which have been folded in half. Label the left side of the paper HORRIBLE. Label the right side with HELPFUL. Ask them to draw a scene of Horace being horrible on the left and then, a revised scene in which he could be helpful instead. Scenes may come from the book, but do encourage students to imagine other horrible/helpful scenes featuring Horace.

Another "Horrible" Book

Share the most famous children's picture book to employ the word "horrible" in its title with your students:

📖 **Book Pairing:** *Alexander and the Terrible, Horrible, No Good, Very Bad Day* by Judith Viorst, illustrated by Ray Cruz. Atheneum, 1972.

In this case, it is not the main character, Alexander, who is horrible, but his day. After you have read the book aloud, ask students to list all of the things that are horrible in Alexander's day. Now ask students to sit quietly and think of the worst day they have ever had. What made their day horrible? List their ideas. Once the list is complete, help them to draw distinctions between those things that are annoyances and those things that are truly challenging and sad.

Hamburger Heaven

**by Wong Herbert Yee.
Houghton Mifflin, 1999.**

Told in rhyming couplets, Hamburger Heaven is the story Pinky Pig, who works at the local hamburger joint to save money for a new clarinet. Unfortunately, business is terrible, and Pinky hatches a plan. When Pinky creates a new line of burgers, crowds respond to the new menu of toppings, which includes caterpillars, crickets, cockroaches, ticks, grasshoppers, ladybugs, and walking sticks. In the end, Pinky's raise is enough to cover the cost of a new clarinet.

Heavenly Hamburger Toppings

Each of the animal townsfolk has a favorite hamburger topping, depending on their usual diet and their animal traits. Begin by asking students to name animals and their favorite special toppings from the book. Once you have a list of animals and their preferences, note that at Hamburger Heaven, every possible topping seems to be fair game.

Now, ask students to use the Heavenly Hamburger Toppings graphic organizer (see page 59) to create their own splendid burger for the menu.

Who's Ordering What?

Tell your students that there are other animals in town that Pinky didn't get a chance to interview for their favorite toppings. Begin by creating a two-column chart, first making a list of all of the wild animals that students can think of who aren't represented in the book. Next, ask students if they know what these animals eat. If you have the time and the appropriate primary reference sources, this will make a fine research project. Assign pairs of students an animal from the class list, and instruct them to do the necessary research to find out what each animal eats.

What Happens to a Hamburger?

You may want to take this opportunity to focus on the human digestive system as you discuss what various animals eat and the topic of hamburgers. Share the following book with students as a thematic tie to Hamburger Heaven with a biological science twist:

📖 **Book Pairing:** *What Happens to a Hamburger?* by Paul Showers, illustrated by Edward Miller. HarperCollins, 2001.

Have a Hamburger

If your school allows occasional sweet treats, host a mock hamburger feast in the library or classroom using this recipe:

- Vanilla wafers (two halves of the bun)
- Small round chocolate mint patties (burger)
- Red and gold decorator frosting in squeeze tubes (catsup and mustard)

Hippo Hide and Seek

Heavenly Hamburger Toppings

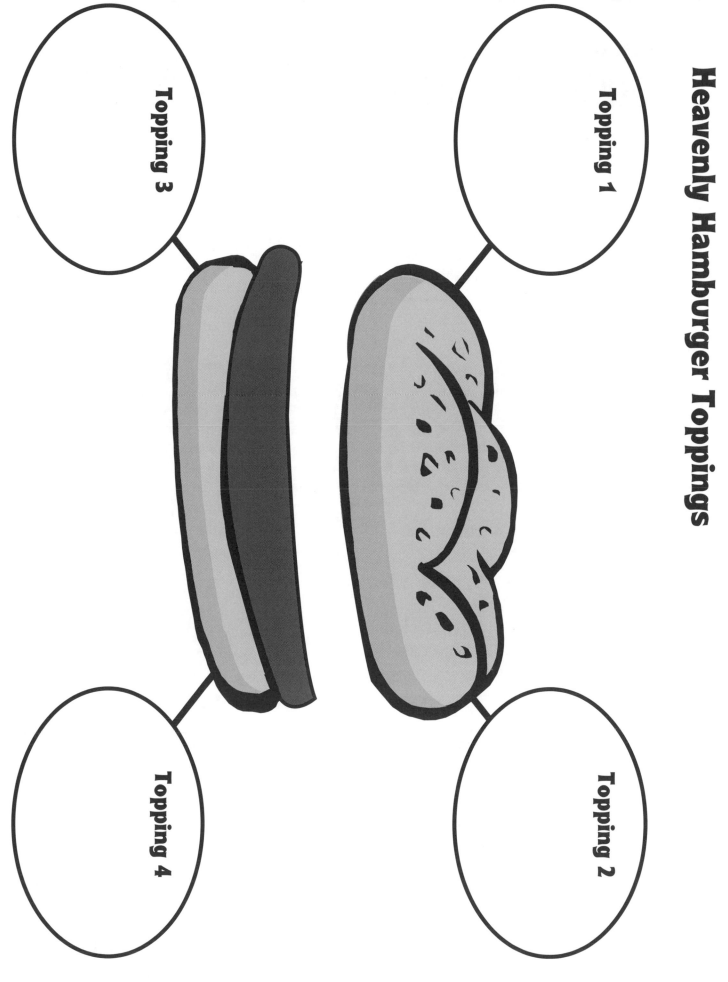

Topping 1

Topping 2

Topping 3

Topping 4

Canine Ice Cream Creations

When Cubby and Spike finally make it to Ice Cream Island, Spike orders a Spumoni Baloney Grande with burger bits swirled in. Ask students to explain why this is the perfect ice cream treat for a dog. Now, invite them to imagine other excellent ice cream treats for both dogs and cats, and to explain why each is particularly suitable.

Ice Cream Fluff

Review the shapes involved in this project before starting the activity. Then, give each student a piece of black construction paper, a long brown triangle (shaped like an ice cream cone), several pieces of polyester batting cut in the shape of a flattened scoop of ice cream, and a glue stick. Invite students to create their own ice cream cone treat and offer them the option to add nuts (lighter brown squares of paper), chocolate (darker brown circles of paper), and cherries (larger red circles) to their cones.

When they have completed the project, ask each student to tell the class about his or her cone using this pattern:

My **triangle** ice cream cone has _____ scoops of **white** vanilla ice cream, _____ **light brown** nut **squares**, _____ **dark brown** chocolate **circles,** and _____ **red** cherry **circles**.

Dream Ice Cream

Using the template on page 64, create a giant ice cream cone and many "scoops" of different colored ice cream for your flannel board. If you don't use a flannel board, try unlined chart paper and glue dots for adhesive.

Review the Flavor/Color correspondences with students. Then, to reinforce color recognition, introduce students to the rhyme:

So many flavors of ice cream to eat, Which flavor will be _____'s special treat?
child's name

As children's names are called, have them announce their favorite flavors from their seats and then come up to stack their favorite flavor pieces on top of the ice cream cone.

Flavor/Color Suggestions

Vanilla—white

Chocolate—brown

Mint—green

Strawberry—pink

Raspberry—red

Orange—orange

Blueberry—blue

Favorite Flavors

After completing the Dream Ice Cream activity, make a chart of the class members' favorite flavors of ice cream. Begin by brainstorming five to seven top flavors of ice cream (don't feel confined to the flavors listed above this time). Create a large graph on chart paper by writing the names of the flavors on the x axis in five (or more) columns. Then, ask students to write their names on one half of an index card, decorate it with a drawing of a small ice cream cone, and place it above the name of their favorite flavor.

Once all votes are posted, discuss the results. For example:

- Which flavor is the most popular?

- Which flavor is the most popular with boys?

- Which flavor is the most popular with girls?

Inch by Inch

by Leo Lionni. Astor-Honor, 1962.

A lucky inchworm is saved from certain death when he tells a hungry robin that he is useful because he measures things. After measuring the robin's tail, the inchworm flies along to measure other birds' anatomy, including the flamingo's neck, the toucan's beak, the heron's legs, the pheasant's tail, and a whole hummingbird. Finally, when the unreasonable nightingale insists that he measure her song, the resourceful inchworm comes up with a plan that saves his life.

Measuring in Units

Explore the concept of linear measurement with your students using rulers. Supply each student with an oversized primary ruler. Discuss the units of measure (foot, inches, portions of inches). Which is the biggest? How many inches are there in a foot? How many half inches in an inch? How many quarter inches in an inch?

Next, introduce the technique of measuring. Demonstrate by measuring the book *Inch by Inch* and reading the final measurement.

Now assign students to work in pairs and measure a variety of items in the room. Have them record their answers on the Measuring in Units graphic organizer on page 63. (Note: For very young students, fill in the names of the items you are requesting that they measure so that they are not required to write them. Adding a drawing of the item will also allow pre-reading students to be more independent.)

We're Going on an Inch Hunt

Once students have been introduced to the primary ruler and measuring with it, invite students, in pairs, to go on a hunt for things that measure an inch or near-to-an-inch in the library or classroom.

To add to the fun, place a bell within reach of all students (on the circulation desk or the teacher's desk) and ask students to ring the bell each time they've been successful in their hunt. When the bell rings, ask all students to pause and the successful team to announce:

A _____ measures one inch. (or A _____ measures a little more/less than an inch.)

"The Garden Song"

If you have already read *How Groundhog's Garden Grew* and completed those activities, your students may be familiar with "The Garden Song" by Dave Mallett. If not, introduce them to this most popular of gardening songs. You can find the words to the song and a midi-file at the KidzSing Garden of Song Web site at www.gardenofsong.com/gardensng.html.

"Inchworm"

Be sure to introduce students to the song "Inchworm" first performed by Danny Kaye in the 1952 movie, Hans Christian Anderson. It is the perfect accompaniment to a reading of *Inch by Inch*. You can find lyrics and a midi-file at the National Institutes of Health, Department of Health & Human Services Web site at kids.niehs.nih.gov/lyrics/inchworm.htm.

> ### I Wanna Iguana
>
> **by Karen Kaufman Orloff, illustrated by David Catrow. Putnam, 2004.**
>
> Alex, the letter-writing main character, pens a note to his mother to let her know that he really ought to take Mikey Gulligan's baby iguana when he moves. His mom, in her response, refuses. Thus begins a series of letters in which Alex tries to convince Mom that iguanas are cuter than hamsters, so small as to be practically unseen, a replacement for the brother he always wanted, and infinitely trainable. In the end, Mom folds!

An Iguana Is the Perfect Pet

Alex makes quite an argument that an iguana is the perfect pet for him. Ask students to list all of the reasons that make an iguana perfect for Alex.

Then, share another perfect-iguana-pet story with your students:

📖 **Book Pairing:** *Mr. Green Peas* by Judith Caseley. Greenwillow Books, 1995.

Ask students to compare the two situations, the two arguments, and the end results.

Iguana Behind Glass

Invite your students to put Mikey Gulligan's baby iguana in a brand-new glass cage in Alex's room.

Give each student crayons, a glue stick, construction paper scraps, a 5x7-inch sheet of light-colored construction paper (to be a "glass" cage), and a cutout of an iguana (see template on page 66). Ask them to color and decorate the iguana cutout first. Then, if they'd like to include plants or rocks in their glass cage, ask them to draw those items on the construction paper, or cut and glue them on from paper scraps. Now, instruct students to glue the cutout to the construction paper background. Finally, complete each glass cage by laying a 5x7 inch sheet of clear contact paper over each student's work.

Name That Iguana

Ask kids to imagine that they are Alex, and Mikey Gulligan's baby iguana has just come to live with them. The first thing they will have to do is to name it. Brainstorm names for the iguana with your students, but inform them that it is a time-honored tradition for iguana names to start with the letter I. Challenge them to think of as many names for the iguana as they can. List them all and then have students vote for their favorite.

Iguana Rap

British children's poet, Brian Moses, has written a wonderful rap poem entitled "Walking with My Iguana." Not only is the text of the poem available on The Poetry Archive Web site at www.poetryarchive.org/poetryarchive/singlePoem.do?poemId=52, but the author reads it aloud with accompanying drums on the site, as well. The recording is not to be missed.

If your students enjoy Moses's rap poem, you can find another, shorter iguana rap poem entitled "Lizard Longing" in Tony Johnston's *I'm Gonna Tell Mama I Want an Iguana* (Putnam, 1990).

> ### Inside, Inside, Inside
>
> **by Holly Meade. Marshall Cavendish, 2005.**
>
> While Mom sleeps in, Noah and his little sister, Jenny, carry on an extended conversation that begins with Jenny finding Noah's blue crystal peewee marble under her bed. When Noah proposes that they empty the salt shaker and put the marble inside, a game of Inside, Inside, Inside begins. Containers are emptied, one after another, and objects are placed inside. Finally, the two create a huge mural of all that is outside the inside objects, to the very edges of the solar system. Mom, of course, wakes up to an enormous mess!

Inside, Inside, Inside

Challenge students to play a game of Inside, Inside, Inside. Of course, as students will have seen in the book, this activity can create quite a mess. Before you begin, discuss the necessity of keeping all of the objects emptied out of various containers in neat, recoverable piles.

Ask students to begin by finding one of the smallest items in the room. Once they've decided on a starting object, take turns in finding another object into which the current item fits (without too much extra space around it). Make sure that each student gets a turn to suggest a container as you proceed to progressively bigger containers. As each item is enclosed, recite the list of items you have encapsulated. For example, the marble is inside the salt shaker which is inside the cereal box which is inside the hat, etc.

Inside, Inside, Inside, Outside Picture

Post a large sheet of craft paper on the wall at child-height, or on the floor as Jenny and Noah do. Now ask students to create an Inside, Inside, Inside, Outside picture. Before you begin, you may want to share a book that will give them a bigger idea of the concept:

📖 **Book Pairing:** *Me on the Map* by Joan Sweeney, illustrated by Annette Cable. Knopf, 1996.

Begin the drawing with the first encased object you created in the Inside, Inside, Inside activity. Now ask questions such as: What room is that inside? What building is that inside? What town is that inside? What state is that inside? What country is that inside? Continue out as far as you like.

Matryoshka Dolls

The ultimate inside, inside, inside toy is a set of Russian matryoshka/matrioshka nesting dolls. Begin by introducing your students to a set of the dolls. If you don't own a set, they are easily obtainable online at Web sites such as www.matrioshka-gift-shop.com or www.russiandollsandboxes.com.

After passing the dolls around and exploring how they work and the concept of "inside" in relation to them, share a matrioshka doll story with your students:

📖 **Book Pairing:** *The Littlest Matryoshka* by Corinne Bliss, illustrated by Kathryn Brown. Hyperion, 1999.

Inside the Box

Obtain a cardboard box large enough to hold two students (or use another container that you already have in your library or classroom). Tell students that they are going to play a two-at-a-time game. Have one student climb into the box and sing "Inside the Box." The class may join in with the singing. In the fifth and sixth line of the song, the student will name the next person to climb in the box. When the second person joins, he or she will sing the song, naming a third student. When the third person is called to come in, the first person exits. Continue through the whole class of students.

"Inside the Box" (sung to the tune of "Frère Jacques")

I am inside.

I am inside,

in a box,

in a box.

_____ is on the outside.

_____ is on the outside.

Come on in.

Come on in.

Dream Ice Cream

Measuring in Units

What We Measured					How Many Inches?

Iguana Behind Glass

Jump, Frog, Jump

by Robert Kalan, illustrated by Byron Barton. Greenwillow Books, 1981.

This cumulative story with a familiar pattern features a fly that climbs out of the water, and a frog that sits under the fly when he climbs out. The fun is enhanced at the end of each section with the lively refrain, "Jump, frog, jump!" The chain backwards from fly and frog goes to a swimming fish, a dropping snake, a sliding turtle, a fishing net, rescuing kids, and a concealing basket. "Jump, frog, jump!"

Exploring Cumulative Tales

Introduce your students to the concept of cumulative tales so that they understand that *Jump, Frog, Jump* is one such story. To reinforce the concept, share another cumulative story with them:

📖 **Book Pairing:** *The House that Jack Built* by Simms Taback. Putnam, 2002.

Ask students to discuss the ways that *The House that Jack Built* and *Jump, Frog, Jump* "work" in the same way. What are the similarities?

Retelling *Jump, Frog, Jump*

Using the templates on pages 70–73, make a set of the characters and props, and mount them on craft sticks or a flannel board. Ask students to retell the story using these props.

Fold a Jumping Frog

The Enchanted Learning Web site has colorful step-by-step instructions for folding an origami jumping frog, a common origami project for children, at www.enchantedlearning. com/crafts/origami/frog. Required materials

are green paper (plan ahead to have this on hand—either origami paper or green copy paper), scissors, and crayons or markers.

Since even origami projects for children require fine motor control, plan to have an older learning buddy on hand for each of your students.

Recite and Sing

The CanTeach Web site has a wonderful collection of frog poems and songs to share with your students at www.canteach.ca/elementary/songspoems59.html.

Joey and Jet

by James Yang. Atheneum, 2004.

Joey's dog Jet is the best ball chaser in the world. He follows the ball no matter where it goes—through a long series of prepositional destinations—until he finally finds it and brings it back to Joey. With retro art and simple text, Joey and Jet will please young readers who will quickly be able to read the book themselves.

Jet Jumps around Town

In this first book of Joey and Jet's adventures, Jet chases his ball all over town. Invite students to make a large map of the town on chart paper, on which the birds, trees, water, hill, street, tables, roofs, and holes are all clearly marked. (Note that the tables and roofs should be a part of other locations such as restaurants and stores.)

Now, using a small model of Jet (bring in a small dog toy or create a cardboard model from the template on page 74), have students recite the story. As they do, have one student at a time put Jet through his moves on the map.

Where Are Joey and Jet Now?

After reading *Joey and Jet*, introduce students to the second book of their adventures:

📖 **Book Pairing:** *Joey and Jet in Space* by James Yang. Atheneum, 2006.

Now, brainstorm Joey and Jet's next adventure. Solicit as many destinations as possible for the team to go to and decide, as a class, which one would be the most fun. Then, ask students to choose one of the two books to use as a model in writing a third book of adventures. (Note: They will choose to create a story in which Jet chases a ball, or where he gets lost.) Once they have chosen the model, write a new Joey and Jet story with simple text and invite students to illustrate each scene.

Just Prepositions

Joey and Jet provides a perfect opportunity to introduce students to prepositions, as Jet goes on a journey to chase his ball in a series of prepositional phrases. First, challenge kids to identify each prepositional phrase, and write it on chart paper.

Then, ask students to help you to create a new list of prepositional phrases that are each introduced in this way:

Jet jumps _____ the _____.
　　　　　　(preposition)　　　　　(noun)

What's in a Name?

Ask students to talk about what a "jet" is. After some discussion, you may want to look up a more formal definition in a primary dictionary such as *Merriam-Webster's Primary Dictionary* by Ruth Heller (2005). Next, read a nonfiction book about jets to broaden student knowledge:

📖 **Book Pairing:** *Jets* by Matt Doeden. Capstone Press, 2007.

Now discuss why Jet is the perfect name for Joey's dog.

Josephina Javelina: A Hairy Tale

by Susan Lowell, illustrated by Bruce MacPherson. Rising Moon, 2005.

Josephina, so different from her brother javelinas Juan and José, longs for the excitement of dancing in the big city. One day, she packs her tutu and concertina and hits the road to Pasadena to join her cousin Angelina. Unfortunately, the talent agent she acquires is a coyote in disguise, who chases the javelinas through the streets of the city and into a parade, where Josephina performs her act and makes her mark. This fame brings her right back home to the Oasis Snack Bar and Cantina.

More than One Way to Pronounce a J

Take this opportunity to discuss the alternate pronunciation of J in Spanish, where it is pronounced like H is in the word, "hot."

With students, make a list of all of the J words in *Josephina Javelina: A Hairy Tale* that are pronounced with the Spanish pronunciation.

What Is a Javelina?

Susan Lowell tells us that javelinas are "hairy, hoggy critters, wild and free." Javelinas are also called "collared peccaries." Begin your research project at the Enchanted Learning Web site where you will find javelina facts and a printable sheet with body parts labeled www.enchantedlearning.com/subjects/mammals/peccary/Javelinaprintout.shtml.

Then, share a nonfiction book about javelinas such as:

📖 **Book Pairing:** *Javelinas* by Conrad Storad. Lerner Publishing Group, 2009.

Javelinas by Lola M. Schaefer. Heinemann Library, 2004.

As you read this nonfiction book, take notes with your students about how javelinas look (physical appearance), where they live (habitat), what they do (behavior), and how they live together (family and young). Record your notes on 5x7" cards or on chart paper. When you have completed your notes, organize them into the four categories and write a short class book about javelinas.

The Three Little Pigs Retold

Susan Lowell's first javelina book is a retelling of *The Three Little Pigs*. Begin this activity by sharing an illustrated version of that tale such as:

📖 **Book Pairing:** *The Three Little Pigs* by Steven Kellogg. HarperCollins, 1997.

Then, read Lowell's book:

📖 **Book Pairing:** *The Three Little Javelinas* by Susan Lowell, illustrated by Jim Harris. Rising Moon, 1992.

Now create a Venn diagram on chart paper or the chalkboard, and ask students to compare the two stories. Be sure to direct students to the differences in setting and characters.

Jumping Javelinas

Invite your students to jump to this jump rope rhyme (using the Spanish pronunciation of the words):

J, my name is Josephina.

My husband's name is Juan.

We are javelinas

And we eat jalepeños.

Retelling *Jump, Frog, Jump* Templates

Retelling Jump, Frog, Jump Templates

Retelling Jump, Frog, Jump Templates

Retelling Jump, Frog, Jump Templates

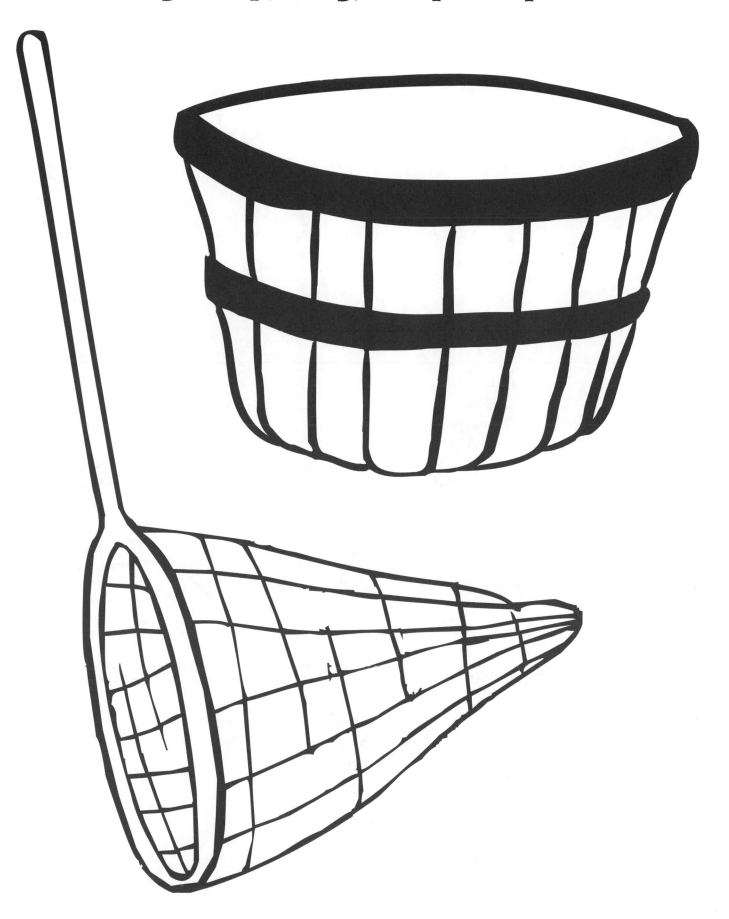

Model of Jet the Dog

Koala Lou

by Mem Fox, illustrated by Pamela Lofts. Gulliver, 1988.

Everyone loves Baby Koala Lou, from the emu to the platypus, to tough little Koala Klaws next door. Mother loves her best, and always makes time to tell her so, until the new brothers and sisters come along. In an effort to remedy the situation, Koala Lou enters the Bush Olympics and competes in the gum tree climbing event. Despite her training and commitment, however, Koala Lou fails to beat Koala Klaws. She does, however, get just what she wanted all along in the sweet words of her mother.

Koala Alikes

Invite students to study the illustrations of *Koala Lou*. Ask whether anyone has ever seen a koala. If so, where? (Note: The zoo or on television are likely responses.) What can they tell you about this unfamiliar animal by looking closely at the illustrations?

Ask students whether the koala reminds them of any other, more familiar animal. If so, which animal? Require them to support their claim by completing the following statement:

A koala reminds me of a _____ because it _____.

Australian K Animals

Koala Lou is an animal from Australia. Using a globe or a flat map of the world, share the location of Australia with your students. Ask them what they notice about Australia. Brainstorm ways that it is different from the United States of America just by looking at the globe or map.

Once they notice that it is surrounded by water (you may want to talk about continents here), you might have a short discussion about how that isolation led to a host of uncommon animals.

Now, introduce the eight Australian animals that begin with K, using the AustralianFauna Web site at www.australianfauna.com/australiananimals.php?id=k.

- Kangaroo Island Dunnart
- Kangaroo (Lumholtz Tree Kangaroo)
- Kangaroo (Red Kangaroo)
- King Parrot
- Kinkajou
- Koala
- Kookaburra
- Kowari

Conduct some primary-level research by projecting the images of these animals using a data projector or electronic whiteboard. Ask students what they notice about each animal, and then share a few facts from the articles.

"The Great Koala Rescue"

Share some live-action footage of a koala from the National Geographic Kids Web site at www.nationalgeographic.com/ngkids/0503/seevideo.html#content. Depending on the developmental level of your students, you may want to share some information with them about the efforts to save the baby koala in this story.

"Cuddly Koalas"

(Sung to the tune of "Frère Jacques.")

Cuddly koalas,
Cuddly koalas.
King parrots too,
King parrots too.
Kinkajou, kowari,
And a kookaburra.
Kangaroos, kangaroos.

The Magic Kerchief

by Kirby Larson, illustrated by Rosanne Litzinger. Holiday House, 2000.

Lonely Griselda lives in solitude just outside of a small village because she speaks her mind—even to Lord Mayor. Her neighbors avoid her; her priest does not pray for her. So she invites a stranger at her door wearing a lovely kerchief to spend the night. In thanks, the old woman gives Griselda her magic kerchief. When Griselda wears it, only compliments and kind words come from her mouth. Of course, once Griselda is kind, her words breed kindness in return.

Wear a Kerchief

Because your students may be unfamiliar with kerchiefs, begin by asking them to discuss what a kerchief is, based on what they see in the illustrations from *The Magic Kerchief*. What does a kerchief look like? How is it worn?

Then, provide them some additional background information on kerchiefs. Historically, they were worn by both men and women. Working men folded them into a triangle and wore them tied around their necks on top of their shirt collars. Women, like Griselda, wore them folded into a triangle over their shoulders (or head and shoulders) and either pinned them or tucked them in front.

Now, give each student a square of cloth of their choice. Together, fold them into triangles and tie them around the neck or shoulders, as each student prefers.

Kerchief Kindness

Once students are wearing their magic kerchiefs, remind them that no matter how much they might want to say something mean or be cranky, the magic kerchief requires them to be kind and friendly to others. Ask students to wear their kerchiefs for a set period of time and then gather them together to report the kind things they've said or done to their class neighbors because of the kerchief magic.

Design a Kerchief

Ask students what Griselda noticed about the stranger's kerchief when the stranger showed up on her doorstep. Perhaps part of the magic of the kerchief was the beauty of the design. Invite students to design their own beautiful kerchief. Provide each student with a large triangle of paper. Ask them to take some time to plan before using markers to draw and color their design on their kerchiefs. Notice that the magic kerchief has flowers on it. Are there other beautiful things from nature that might also make good decorations?

When the kerchiefs are complete, gather students to share and discuss why they chose the designs they did for their kerchiefs.

"Magic Kerchief"

Teach students the lyrics to this song, sung to the tune of "Frère Jacques."

"Magic Kerchief"

Magic kerchief,
Magic kerchief,
That I wear,
That I wear.
I can say a kind word.
I can do a good deed.
I can share.
I can share.

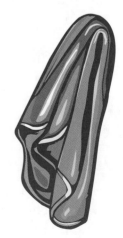

> ### *Kittens! Kittens! Kittens!*
>
> **by Susan Meyers, illustrated David Walker. Abrams, 2007.**
>
> Following newborn kittens as they grow, develop, and explore their surroundings, this extended, lilting rhyming poem tells a great deal about the furry pets while employing delicious language throughout.

What Do Kittens Do?

Remind students that verbs are action words in a story. Re-read *Kittens! Kittens! Kittens!* and look for action words that describe what the kittens are doing, such as nestling, standing up, and growing. Once you have a comprehensive list of the verbs that Meyers uses in her text, challenge students to think of additional verbs that describe real kitten behavior.

Kitten Care

Suggest that your students write a kitten care book based on the information they've learned from *Kittens! Kittens! Kittens!* What do kittens do? What do they need? Of course, the guide will be illustrated, so invite students to choose the piece of advice they'd most like to render artistically.

For additional ideas, you may want to read a nonfiction kitten care book such as:

📖 **Book Pairing:** *Kitten Care: A Guide to Loving and Nurturing Your Pet* by Kim Dennis-Bryan. DK Publishing, 2004.

"Three Little Kittens"

Begin by reading a picture book version of the classic nursery rhyme, "Three Little Kittens."

📖 **Book Pairing:** *Three Little Kittens* by Lori-anne Siomades. Boyds Mills Press, 2000.

Now teach your students to recite the rhyme:

Three little kittens,
They lost their mittens,
And they began to cry,
Oh, mother dear,
We sadly fear
Our mittens we have lost.
What! Lost your mittens,
You naughty kittens!
Then you shall have no pie.
Mee-ow, mee-ow, mee-ow, mee-ow.
You shall have no pie.

The three little kittens,
They found their mittens,
And they began to cry,
Oh, mother dear,
See here, see here,
Our mittens we have found.
What! Found your mittens,
You darling kittens!
Then you shall have some pie.
Mee-ow, mee-ow, mee-ow, mee-ow.
You shall have some pie.

The three little kittens,
Put on their mittens,
And soon ate up the pie;
Oh, mother dear,
We greatly fear
Our mittens we have soiled.
What! Soiled your mittens,
You naughty kittens!
Then they began to sigh,
Mee-ow, mee-ow, mee-ow, mee-ow.
They began to sigh.

The three little kittens,
They washed their mittens,
And hung them out to dry;
Oh mother dear,
Look here, look here,
Our mittens we have washed.
What! Washed your mittens,
You're such good kittens.
I smell a rat close by!
Hush! Hush! Hush! Hush!
Hush! Hush! Hush!
I smell a rat close by.

Three Little Flannel Kittens

Create an easy flannel board set using the templates on page 78. Allow students to take turns at the board enacting the poem using the flannel pieces, and being a part of the reciting audience, as well.

If you'd also like a rebus version of the nursery rhyme, visit the Enchanted Learning Web site at www.enchantedlearning.com/rhymes/ Threelittlekittens.shtml.

Flannel Kittens

Little Loon and Papa

by Toni Buzzeo, illustrated by Margaret Spengler. Dial, 2004.

Papa Loon wants to teach his little loon to dive, but Little Loon is nervous. As Papa gently dips and tips him, Little Loon resists. When Papa zips under the water to model, his baby escapes and gets lost. After encountering a trio of northwoods animals, Little Loon finds his courage, and dives to reach his papa.

What Makes a Loon a Loon?

Students often confuse loons with ducks, especially if they do not live in the small swath of northern states where common loons live. To teach students more about this water bird, read an article from a primary level encyclopedia such as *Discovery Encyclopedia* (2009), or excerpts from a nonfiction book about loons such as:

📖 **Book Pairing:** *Loons: Diving Birds of the North* by Donna Love, illustrated by Joyce Mihran Turley. Mountain Press, 2003.

Encourage students to help you list facts that make loons unique.

Listen to Loon Talk

Explain to students that the common loon has four distinct calls: the hoot, the yodel, the tremolo, and the wail. The hoot is used between members of a family group or flock when they are maintaining close contact. In *Little Loon and Papa*, Papa Loon hoots at Little Loon. The yodel is a call used only by males who are setting boundaries or fighting. The tremolo is used by both males and females

when they are frightened. Finally, the wail is used when loons are trying to maintain contact at a distance or trying to locate a mate or chick. In *Little Loon and Papa*, Papa Loon wails when Little Loon is lost. Loon chicks have only one call, which is a peent. Little Loon peents throughout the book.

Share the sounds of these four loon calls from the Loon Preservation Committee Web site www.loon.org/multimedia.htm. Ask students to imagine what the loon might say in words each time it uses one of its calls.

Little Loon's Lessons

Explain to your students how loons dive. According to loon biologists, adult loons first expel all of the air from their lungs and air sacs inside their bodies. Next, they tuck their waterproof feathers close against their bodies, forcing out all the air trapped between them. Then, they sink below the surface because unlike most other birds with hollow bones, loons have many solid bones, which help this process. When diving, loons move only their feet, not their wings, to propel them through the water. (Note: Because baby loons have fluff rather than feathers, they must use their wings as well as their feet to launch themselves beneath the surface of the water.) So when Papa dives under water, the text reads:

SQUEEZE

TUCK

ZIP!

Papa disappears from sight.

Once students understand the mechanics of loon diving, invite them, as a group, to listen to *Little Loon and Papa* again and then write a set of instructions that Papa Loon might have given to Little Loon to teach him to dive.

Lessons Learned

After reading *Little Loon and Papa* and completing the Little Loon's Lessons activity above, ask students to think of something that one of their parents has taught them to do, such has riding a bike, paddling a canoe, or washing the dishes. Ask them to tell, step by step, the instructions for completing the activity. Using ordinal numbers (first, second, third) may be helpful in describing the correct chronology of actions.

This Land is Your Land

by Woody Guthrie, illustrated Kathy Jakobsen. Little, Brown and Company, 1998.

A beautifully illustrated rendering of the famous Woody Guthrie song brings the folk song to life as the reader travels across the United States. A complete set of lyrics take the reader through hard times and social injustice as well as pretty landscape.

Singing the Book

You may have a copy of *This Land is Your Land* with an enclosed recording of Woody Guthrie singing this and other songs. If you do not, you can find words and lyrics at the National Institutes of Health, Department of Health & Human Services Web site at <u>kids.niehs.nih.gov/lyrics/thisland.htm</u>. Practice singing the song together and consider performing it at a school-wide assembly.

What Is a Land?

With your students, explore the various meanings of the word "land." Begin by soliciting their definitions of the word, and then clarify even further by consulting a primary level dictionary, such as *Merriam-Webster's Primary Dictionary* by Ruth Heller (2005). Emphasize the concept of a land as a country where a nation makes its home. Explain that the land that Woody Guthrie was writing about was the whole United States.

Invite students to create an illustration of one place in the United States that they have visited. Some students will not have been out of their neighborhood, town, or state, but others will have traveled far. Ask those who have traveled to choose somewhere they have been. On a bulletin board or wall, display student illustrations with a short sentence identifying the place pictured and a caption reading THIS LAND WAS MADE FOR YOU AND ME.

Walk Across the Land

Post a large map of the United States and gather as many clues as possible from the text and illustrations to mark each place that the song's narrator visits in this land of ours.

If time allows, invite students to explore the state books in the nonfiction section of the library to find photographs of the places you mark on the map.

Saving the Land

While sharing *This Land is Your Land* with students, take the opportunity to discuss ways to be good environmental stewards of the land. Begin by reading a book that celebrates life on planet Earth:

📖 **Book Pairing:** *Our Big Home: An Earth Poem* by Linda Glaser, illustrated by Elisa Kleven. Millbrook Press, 2000.

Then, as a class, brainstorm ways that we can be actively involved in keeping the land (and water) clean, safe, and, in the case of water, plentiful. Finally, enact some of their ideas. For instance, you may decide to take a trash walk, particularly through a natural setting such as a woods or a park, if this is possible; or start a recycling program at your school. Empower your students to make a difference!

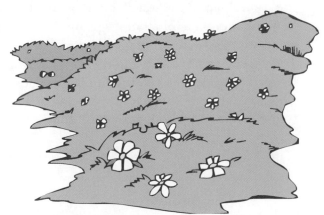

Library Lion

by Michelle Knudsen, illustrated by Kevin Hawkes. Candlewick Press, 2006.

When a lion walks into the public library, the librarian, Miss Merriweather, has no rules to prohibit his presence, so he stays and becomes a part of the life and workings of the library. However, when Miss Merriweather falls and the lion must get Mr. McBee's attention, he is forced to roar, thus breaking a rule and finding himself banished from the library. Luckily, after a long and lonely time, Mr. McBee finds the lion and informs him that the unfortunate rule has been changed.

"Library Song"

Teach your students the Michael Mark and Tom Chapin song, "Library Song." Lyrics can be found at the Songs for Teaching Web site at http://www.songsforteaching.com/tomchapin/librarysong.htm where you can also find a sound clip to teach you the tune or an option to buy the Moonboat CD on which it appears.

Library Rules

Ask students to think about the rules in the school library. List them and discuss the reasons behind them. If your students have been to the public library, ask them about any rules there that might be different from the school library rules. Add those to your list and discuss the reasons behind them.

Now imagine that you were revising the list of rules for your school and/or public library, because lions are going to be regular users of the library. Ask students to think of some rules it would be necessary to add to the list (for instance, one rule suggestion might be, Keep your tail from swinging near the shelves unless you are dusting.)

Lion Library Work

In *Library Lion*, the lion takes on some regular jobs in the library, including dusting the encyclopedias, licking envelopes, and acting as a stepstool for small children at the bookshelves. Ask students to think about the work of all kinds that is done in the school library. If the lion came to your school, what are the many jobs that he could do to help out?

Invite each student to think of a job and then illustrate the lion doing it. If you have time, encourage students to write Lion a short letter that begins:

Dear Lion,

I would like to invite you to my library so that you can _____.

What Do Real Lions Do?

Ask students what makes *Library Lion* such a silly story. They will know it is inherently silly, because lions can't really spend their days in the library or be helpful there. Ask them where lions actually live and how they behave in real life. Make a list of their ideas and then lead them on an exploration to find additional facts about real lion habitat and behavior.

Start by sharing the video about lion habitat and behavior at the National Geographic Kids Creature Feature Web site at kids.nationalgeographic.com/Animals/CreatureFeature/Lion.

Then, read one or more nonfiction books about lions such as:

📖 **Book Pairing:** *A Lion Grows Up* by Anastasia Suen, illustrated by Michael L. Denman and William J Huiett. Picture Window Books, 2006.

Lions by Jill Anderson. NorthWord, 2006.

Look Some More

After you have read *Look! Look! Look!* aloud to students, bring in a stack of art postcards for them to view individually or in small groups. Ask them to LOOK closely at the cards and identify colors, lines, patterns, and shapes as the mice do in the book. You may want to provide small frames like the ones the mice use to focus their view.

One interesting option if you don't have access to paper postcards is to use Art Postcards online at www.artpostcard.com. You can select by style, subject, country, or keyword and then project the images you choose using an electronic whiteboard or a data projector. Another option is to choose several art books from the nonfiction collection in the library.

Look at the Lines

Ask each student to choose one art image/painting from the Look Some More activity above. (Note: Paintings with a single figure, object, or still life will work much better than landscapes.) Re-read the section of *Look! Look! Look!* that describes the mice rendering the image of the woman only in line. Suggest that they begin with a single color marker on a blank sheet of paper, and make the line that would serve as the outline of the person or object in the painting. Next, using a second color, ask them (or a partner) to draw a set of interior lines. Finally, using a third color, instruct them (or another partner) to draw a second set of interior lines.

A Looking Walk

Invite students to join you on a looking walk around the school or the neighborhood with a pencil and a sketchbook in hand. Teach them to make a "frame" with their thumbs and forefingers to narrow their field of vision. Periodically, stop in place, ask students to frame something with their hands, and then ask them to sketch what they see in their finger frames.

"Look, Look, Look at Art"

Sing this song to the tune of "Row, Row, Row Your Boat." Once students know the words, you may also want to try it as a round.

Look, look, look at art
colors, shapes, and line.

Carefully, carefully you can see
if you just take your time.

Look, look, look at art
frame in what you see.

When you look more closely there,
you'll see as much as me.

The Missing Mitten Mystery

by Steven Kellogg. Dial, 2000.

Annie has already lost FIVE mittens this winter. She's in big trouble, so she and her dog Oscar go on a hunt for the missing mitten, checking each place they have played during the day. While revisiting the fun they've had, they find a pile of missing winter clothing articles—but no red mitten. Finally, at Miss Seltzer's house, as the sun sets, Annie imagines planting a mitten tree in the garden. When a cold rain begins to fall, Annie and Miss Seltzer enjoy a cup of hot chocolate and find the mysterious lost mitten.

What Can a Mitten Be?

Revisit the story with the class and make a list of all of the things that Annie thought were her mitten (such as a flying cardinal), and all of the things she imagined her mitten could be (such as a mummy costume for a mouse). Now invite students to use their imaginations to come up with other things that might be mistaken for a red mitten, and other imagined uses for it. Ask each student to select one idea and draw it.

Missing Object Mysteries

Ask students what a mystery is. Share the definition of "mystery" from a good primary dictionary such as *Merriam-Webster's Primary Dictionary* by Ruth Heller (2005). If students are familiar with the use of the dictionary, ask them where they think you might find the word "mystery" in the dictionary to reinforce their location skills.

Discuss the mystery in *The Missing Mitten Mystery*, and then ask students whether they have ever experienced a missing item mystery. As students think of a time when something they owned was missing, invite the class to come up with ideas of where that item might have gone. Once students have heard enough ideas generated about the missing objects, ask them to use the Mystery Solved graphic organizer on page 87 to illustrate the object's whereabouts by choosing the best solution to the mystery. Students will draw a picture of the missing item in the oval, and then illustrate the mystery solution.

Mittens Mounting

If you live in a cold climate, your students are well aware of the problem of lost mittens and gloves. Begin by reading another missing mitten story:

📖 **Book Pairing:** *A Mountain of Mittens* by Lynn Plourde, illustrated by Mitch Vane. Charlesbridge, 2007.

Discuss the solutions that the parents in this story employed to keep the kids and their mittens together. Would any of these solutions have worked for Annie? Why or why not?

Now, if your climate is appropriate, ask each student to bring in one pair of mittens. Graph the mittens by color to determine whether Annie's red mittens are the most popular color in your class.

Sing and Recite Mittens

Invite your students to memorize a few mitten poems. You will find an excellent collection at the CanTeach Web site at www.canteach.ca/elementary/songspoems33.html.

Mother's Day Mice

by Eve Bunting, illustrated by Jan Brett. Clarion, 1986.

Biggest Mouse, Middle Mouse, and Little Mouse sneak out into the early morning on Mother's Day to find Mother a gift. The older siblings are dismissive of Little Mouse's plan to get Mother honeysuckle, because Cat lives at Honeysuckle Cottage. Even though Cat prevents Little Mouse from picking honeysuckle, inside the cottage someone is playing a tune on the piano. He brings an even better gift—a song he creates from the piano music he hears.

A Gift for Mother

Ask students to think about gifts they might choose to give their own mothers, grandmothers, or aunts. Begin by allowing each child to list one thing. Once you have recorded these ideas, go through the list and circle all of the ideas that begin with M. Now, challenge students to add as many more ideas as they can that begin with M.

Hidden Gifts

Give each student a large paper plate that has been divided into four quadrants with a marker. Ask them to draw each of the mice's gifts in a quadrant: strawberry, dandelion fluff, song (however they would like to represent that) in the first three, and then one of the M gifts from the list above in the fourth quadrant. Place another paper plate with the fourth quadrant cut out over each student's plate, and fasten with a brad in the middle.

Ask students to relate the story of the gifts, one at a time, using this script:

First, Middle Mouse picked mother a round, red strawberry for Mother's Day.

Then, Biggest Mouse picked mother a dandelion fluff ball for Mother's Day.

Finally, Littlest Mouse sang Mother a song for Mother's Day.

But I'd give my mother/grandmother/aunt a _____ for Mother's Day.

"Little Mouse's Song"

Even before you read the book aloud, you will probably want to combine "Little Mouse's Song" with music so that you can sing it when you arrive at that page in the story. It sings quite nicely to the tune of "Twinkle Twinkle, Little Star" if you repeat the first two lines of the song at the end.

Once you have sung the song in the context of the story, teach it to your students and sing it aloud together.

Sing a Song for Mothers

Challenge your students to select another well-known children's tune and create another Mother's Day song to accompany the music. "Row, Row, Row Your Boat" is an interesting choice if the first two lines are:

Sing, sing, sing a song

On this Mother's Day.

How might students suggest completing that song?

Mysterious Moles

After reading *Mole Music*, ask students what they think they may know about moles. Ask them to explain why they are drawing this conclusion. Make a list of student conclusions and then do some research on moles by sharing a nonfiction book with the class.

📖 **Book Pairing:** *Moles* by Patricia Whitehouse. Heinemann, 2004.

After reading about moles, determine whether the conclusions made were true or false. Ask each student who made a comment to reevaluate his or her statement for accuracy.

Mole Holes

Mole lives underground in a series of tunnels that he digs for himself. After students examine Mole's home and look carefully at other illustrations of mole burrows, ask them to pretend that they are mole architects and design an excellent mole home underground consisting of connected tunnels.

Music that Moves You

Mole makes music that is so moving, it stops wars and changes the world. Open a discussion with students about the things that music can make you feel. Ask students to talk about different kinds of music and how they feel when

listening to it. Then, make the experience real by playing a variety of music, from finger-snapping to solemn (and be sure to include a piece with a wonderful violin). After playing a snippet of each piece, ask students to talk about how it makes them feel.

"Mole Plays the Violin"

(Sung to the tune of "The Farmer in the Dell.")

Mole plays the violin.
Tucked up beneath his chin
Hi-ho the derry-o,
Mole plays the violin.

Mole lives beneath the ground.
But his music travels 'round.
Hi-ho the derry-o,
Mole lives beneath the ground.

Mole's music stops the war.
It makes good feelings soar.
Hi-ho the derry-o,
Mole's music stops the war.

Celebrating Mud

After reading *Mud* aloud to the class, open a discussion of students' personal experiences with mud. What do they remember? Lead them to focus on the five senses with these questions:

- How did it feel?
- How did it smell?
- What did you hear?
- What did you see?
- You didn't taste it, did you?

Make a list of the phrases they used to describe their sensory experiences with mud. From these phrases, write one or more class mud poems.

You Didn't Taste It, Did You?

After you complete your Celebrating Mud activity, remind students of that final sensory question: You didn't taste it, did you? Tell them that even though it seems like a silly question, they will be able to answer YES at the end of this activity.

Invite students to help you make mud pudding. Prepare instant chocolate or butterscotch pudding according to the recipe and spoon it into five ounce paper cups. Now allow students to spruce up their mud by spooning in crushed chocolate cookies, gummy worms of various colors, and raisins.

When all mixing and eating is complete, ask students, "You didn't taste it, did you?" and expect a resounding "Yes!"

"I Love Mud"

Maine singer-songwriter Rick Charette's song, "I Love Mud" is a perfect accompaniment to a reading of *Mud*. Introduce your students to the lyrics of the song and help them to memorize it. (Note: Memorizing the chorus will take no more than sixty seconds, and you can expect raucous chanting of it thereafter!) You can find the lyrics to the song online at www.pinepoint. com/Lyrics/I_Love_Mud_lyrics.html, but you may need to borrow or buy Charette's *Alligator in the Elevator* album in order to learn the melody, unless you are familiar with the song.

Reading in a Mud Puddle

Using brown craft paper, design a "mud puddle" big enough to hold a class of students. As they enter the story area, tell them that they must be very careful not to splash the mud from the puddle around the room. When everyone is settled, read a trio of other mud stories to the group.

📖 **Book Pairing:** *Mud Puddle* by Robert Munsch, illustrations by Sami Suomalainen. Annick, 1995.

Pigs in the Mud in the Middle of the Rud by Lynn Plourde, illustrated by John Schoenherr. Down East, 2006.

Stuck in the Mud by Jane Clarke, illustrations by Garry Parsons. Walker & Co., 2008.

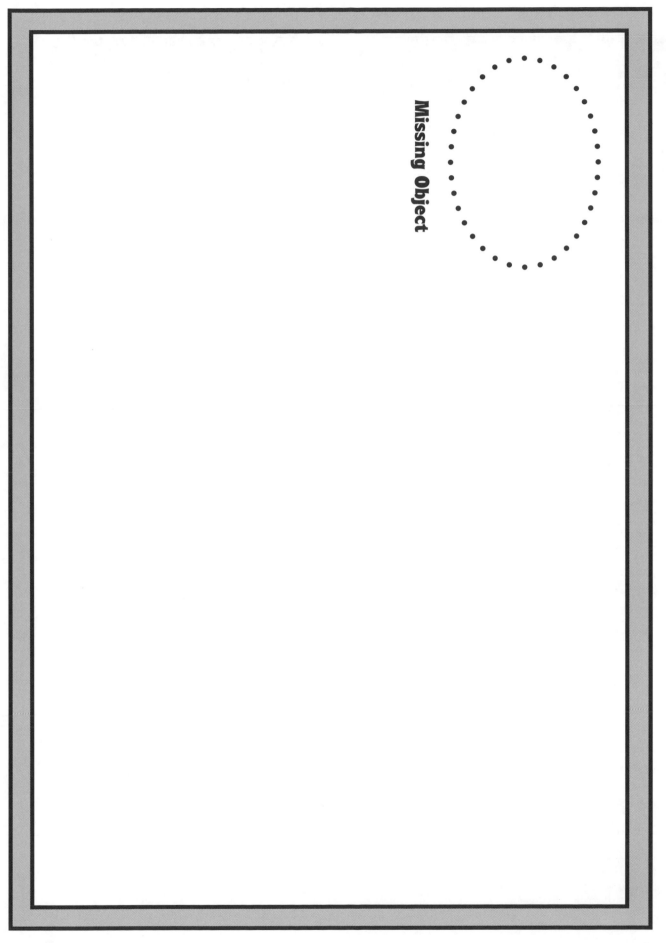

Missing Object

Not Norman

by Kelly Bennett, illustrated by Noah Z. Jones. Candlewick Press, 2005.

On his birthday, the narrator, who hoped for a soft and furry pet who could run and catch, instead receives Norman, a sorry looking fish in a bowl. He decides to trade him in, but first, he cleans his bowl (and Norman is happy). He takes him to school (and Norman pays attention to his presentation). Norman sings along with his tuba playing. Norman even calms him when he's scared. When he gets to the pet store on Saturday, he finds lots of great pets, but none as great as Norman.

Measuring Up

Engage kids in a conversation about what makes a good pet. Ask them to think about the text, and talk about the qualities that the narrator was wishing for in a pet. Then, open the discussion to include additional qualities that they personally value in a pet. From the conversation, generate a list of desirable pet qualities and write them on a chart, leaving space at the right side for two columns, marked NORMAN and NOT NORMAN.

Once the list is complete, read each item and ask kids to say, "Norman," or "Not Norman" based on whether the quality applies to the fish.

Design a Fish

After completing the Measuring Up activity, ask students to choose one quality that is "Not Norman" and redesign Norman so that he has that quality. Discuss what might be required. For instance, for Norman to run and jump, he'd need two, or even four legs. For him to cuddle up on your lap, he'd need lungs and nostrils for breathing air.

Ask students to draw their redesigned Norman and to include a caption that says, "Norman can _____." Display the pictures on a bulletin board.

Norman at Night

One night, the narrator of *Not Norman* gets scared. Ask students to explain what scares him. When they mention the screeching sound, explore why that sound is scary. Be sure to discuss the role that imagination plays in the creation of fear. Next, explore why Norman is not scared. Children may suppose that goldfish cannot hear, but in fact, you may assure students that much research has been done on goldfish by scientists who have proven that they do hear.

Narrator, Narrator!

Not Norman provides a perfect opportunity to talk about first-person narration. Ask students who is telling the story. They are likely to talk about the boy they see in the pictures, because a picture book provides visual clues to the narrator's physical traits and actions. Read the first page of the book aloud again. Now ask students to change the story to third-person narration, replacing the "I" with a boy's name, and then "he," when that pronoun is appropriate. Ask the class who the narrator is now.

Next, tell students a very short story about what you had for breakfast. Then, ask them to render your first-person story in third person. Give students a chance to do this activity in pairs, emphasizing that they are changing the NARRATOR of the story.

Night Noises: House or Neighborhood?

Some noises that the narrator hears are inside, household noises. Ask students to list examples of these from the story. Other noises he hears are outside noises from the street or the weather. Ask students to list examples of these from the story, as well.

Now share another story of night noises with your students and ask them to repeat the instructions:

📖 **Book Pairing:** *The Night is Singing* by Jacqueline Davies, illustrated by Kyrsten Brooker. Dial, 2006.

Display a list of all of the night noises from the two stories. Ask students to illustrate the list if you like.

Noisy Adventures

The narrator and his dog in *Noises at Night* hear many noises in their house and neighborhood as they are trying to fall asleep. Invite students to think of the noises they hear when they are trying to fall asleep at night. As they relate each noise, try first to capture the spelling of the noise as the authors did in the book, with extended consonant and vowel sounds that form onomatopoeias.

Write each child's sound statement on his or her drawing paper, using the first line of each adventure page in the book as a model. Now ask each student to imagine what adventure their sound could turn into. Invite them to draw the picture of themselves participating in that adventure.

Especially at Night

At night, we experience many things in a more intense way. For instance, in *Noises at Night*, the young narrator hears sounds more clearly. In addition to sharper hearing, we might see certain things, such as stars, more clearly, or we might feel certain emotions more keenly. Talk with your students about the night. What makes it special? What do they like best about nighttime? Record their comments and ideas on a list for the class to reference, and then create an "Especially at Night" class poem. You might want to use this line format:

In _____'s night, the _____ sings
    (name)   (noun)

(or another verb). Ending with: In everyone's night, sleep carries us away.

"Noise, Noise, Noise at Night"

Remind students of the tune to "Row, Row, Row Your Boat," perhaps by singing it one time through.

Now introduce them to this night noises version. When they are accomplished at it, consider singing in the round:

Noise, noise, noise at night,

What can it all be?

Dripping and snapping and popping and tapping,

I want to go to sleep!

A Nutty Feast

In the back matter, author Lois Ehlert tells us that gray squirrels like to eat acorns, hickory nuts, walnuts, beechnuts, and pecans, as well as maple seeds, pine seeds, corn, and fruit. After ascertaining that none of the students is allergic to nuts, host a nutty feast for the class by offering samples of a selection of these nuts. (Note: acorns can be ordered online if you feel adventurous.)

Generate a math activity from the tasting by listing the varieties of nuts you have available on chart paper, and then graphing the favorite nuts of the group. Tally votes by inviting students to attach a squirrel sticker in the appropriate column.

Nuts Underground

Also in the back matter, author Lois Ehlert tells us that squirrels bury nuts underground by digging with their front feet. Later, the squirrels return to find them. She explains that they do not find the nuts by memory, but rather, they locate their hoards using their exceptional sense of smell.

If your school has indoor or outdoor sandboxes, challenge your students to bury—and then find—walnuts in the same way that squirrels do. Begin by giving each student a gray squirrel mask to color and wear (see template on page 92). Then, give each student a walnut with his or her initials written on the shell in permanent marker. Instruct them to bury the walnuts in the sandbox. Allow some time to pass (perhaps hold the Nutty Feast at this point), and then return to the sandbox. Challenge students, one at a time, to dig up the walnut with their personal initials on it.

"I'm a Nut"

Visit the Songs for Teaching Web site at www. songsforteaching.com/hughhanley/imanut. htm to learn Hugh Hanley's "I'm a Nut" chant, and to view the photographs of the body motions that accompany it. You will also find a link to an excerpt of Hanley performing a portion of the piece to get you started.

"Five Little Walnuts"

Invite students to use their fingers to count down the walnuts as they chant.

Five little walnuts hanging by the door.

One fell down and then there were four.

Four little walnuts hanging from our tree.

One fell off and then there were three.

Three little walnuts stuck like glue.

One fell off and then there were two.

Two little walnuts hanging in the sun.

One fell off and then there was one.

One little walnut—now we're nearly done.

It fell off and then there were none.

N Is for Neighbor

Begin a discussion with your students about what a neighbor is. Is it just a person who lives right next door, like Mr. Robinson does to Nicholas? Or is it anyone who lives on your street? Or might it even be anyone who lives in your whole neighborhood? There is no single correct answer, of course.

Now ask students to name their favorite "good neighbor" (of any age), and describe what makes him or her a favorite. Invite students to draw a picture of these favorite neighbors, and create a bulletin board or wall display.

"Won't You Be My Neighbor?"

PBS television star Fred Rogers composed the most famous children's song about neighbors and sang it regularly on his "Mr. Rogers' Neighborhood" television show. Find the lyrics and music for "Won't You Be My Neighbor?" on the PBS Kids Web site at pbskids.org/rogers/songlist/song1.html. If students don't know the words, teach them the song and sing it together.

Any N Name

Both Nicholas and his sister, Nina, have names that begin with N. Starting with name examples from your own class, brainstorm a list of human first names beginning with N. Now brainstorm a list of human last names that begin with N. Then, have fun combining the first and last names to create interesting character names for a new story about neighbors that you devise as a class.

Of course, Nicholas's dog's name, Bitsy, does not begin with N, but your students may be able to think of some dog names that do to add more fun to the story.

"New Neighbors"

(Sung to the tune of "Row, Row, Row Your Boat.")

New new new neighbors
Living right next door,

Come outside and play with me
There's so much to explore.

New new new neighbors
Living right next door,

We will have a lot more fun
Than you've ever had before.

Nuts Underground

Staple elastic
band here

Staple elastic
band here

Cut

Cut

Cut

Butterflies for Kiri

**by Cathryn Falwell.
Lee & Low Books, 2003.**

Because Kiri loves to create things, her Auntie Lu sends her a box of special papers and a book on origami for her birthday. Kiri loves the thin, beautiful papers and reads the book with its interesting folding directions, but her first attempt to make an origami butterfly is a mess. She turns instead to other paper art, but again encounters feelings of failure. However, she discovers that using her origami paper to create collage illustration solves the problem, and also gives her the courage to fold it into a beautiful butterfly.

What Is Origami?

After you read the article entitled "Origami Origins" at web.archive.org/web/20001008002845/http://ccwf.cc.utexas.edu/~vbeatty/exhibit_archive/origami1/history/origins.html, share a simplified history of origami with your students. Using a world map or globe, show students the locations of China and Japan as you explain this history.

Fold an Animal

As we see in *Butterflies for Kiri*, origami can be frustrating for small hands, especially when using very thin origami paper. So make plans for origami folding that will allow your young students to experience success. First, be sure to use heavier weight origami paper designed for children. Second, begin with an exceptionally simple origami project such as the:

- Simple Origami Butterfly
- Simple Origami Jumping Frog
- Simple Origami Whale

Directions for all three animals available at the Enchanted Learning Web site at www.enchantedlearning.com/crafts/origami.

Third, if possible, invite an older class of students to partner with your young students on the project. Be sure that the older students have an opportunity to create the origami project themselves, first, and then provide guidelines for acting as buddies for the younger students in the project.

Original Art

Generate a conversation with students about Kiri's "original" art. When she visits the park and is inspired to paint her own impression of the springtime scene, she is making original art, which she finds deeply satisfying. Invite your students to create their own original artistic scene that might include a butterfly, jumping frog, or whale. Then, after they complete one of the origami shapes above, include it in their painting or drawing.

Fold a Poem

Share this wonderful origami and poetry book with your students:

📖 **Book Pairing:** *Fold Me a Poem* by Kristine O'Connell George, illustrated by Lauren Stringer. Harcourt, 2005.

Then, invite your students to create a poem about an imagined origami figure they might create. If you have additional help available, use print and online origami resources to find instructions for folding the imagined figure.

In addition, you will find a fabulous download-able Teacher's Guide to accompany this book at the author's Web site at www.kristinegeorge. com/teachers_guide_fold_me_a_poem.html.

Your Unique Neighborhood

After you read *Only One Neighborhood* aloud, ask students to think of things there are only one of in your neighborhood (or town, if you live in a small enough town). Consider these possibilities: library, pharmacy, grocery store, tailor, bank, hospital, police station, sewage treatment plant, waterworks, hardware store, post office, lumber-yard, gas station, museum. Once students have exhausted their list of places in the neighbor-hood, fill out a t-chart that looks like this:

Only One _____	But many _____ inside

Only One with Many Parts

Ask students to think about the "only one" concept beyond the neighborhood organizer. What other singular things can they think of that contain many items? Encourage students to think of things that are a single collection with many parts. For instance, each child may have only one BOX of crayons, but inside

there are many crayons. Mom may have one KEYRING, but on it are many keys. Other examples might include a package of gum, a roll of candy, a beehive, a flock of geese, an ant hill, etc.

Only One Wish

At the end of *Only One Neighborhood*, Harshman and Garrison tell us that all countries in the world have only one wish: peace. Discuss the idea of only one wish with students and ask them to think about what their only wish might be if they were granted just ONE. At first, children may think of toys they want or things they like to eat, but you may want to lead them to think about more abstract wishes that neverthe-less apply to their own lives.

Ask each child to create an illustration of his or her wish come true. Label the wish with the child's name and display them on a bulletin board or wall.

"There's Only One Me"

Recite this poem with your children.

There are ____ children in my class, (number of children in the class)

from _____ to _____ . (first and last names, in alphabetical order)

Each one is special,

and each is unique,

but—

there's only one me,

only one me,

I'm the only one

there will ever be!

The Perfect Pet

by Margie Palatini, illustrated by Bruce Whatley. HarperCollins, 2003.

Elizabeth really, really, really wants a pet. Her parents really, really, really do not, so they give her a cactus, which Elizabeth names Carolyn. But when it becomes clear that Carolyn lacks the essential cuddle factor, Elizabeth begins a campaign to convince her parents to let her have a different pet. Elizabeth has no luck until she finds Doug, a bug. At long last, Elizabeth has a pet, and her parents finally make peace with the fact.

Pet Round Up

Ask students to discuss their feelings about pets. Do any students have a pet at home? Do any students want a pet who don't already have one? Do any students have more than one pet?

Now, list all the different types of pets that students have in a vertical list on chart paper. Once the list is complete, create two columns next to the list. Label one I OWN ONE and label the second column I WANT ONE (to ensure that all students get to participate). Then, proceed by calling on one child at a time, or, more simply, one pet at a time. Tally responses in each column to determine the most popular pets.

Your Perfect Pet

Begin by making a list of the pets that Elizabeth tried to talk her parents into. Then, invite students to think of the perfect pet they would like to convince their own parents to allow them to have. Ask each student to support his or her choice. Why is this pet the PERFECT pet for him or her? Once children have defended their perfect pets, ask them to draw themselves at home, having fun with their pet and their family members.

Design a Pet

It is possible that the truly perfect pet is a cross between many different pets, such as a furry fish, a galloping frog, or a bat-winged, flying kitten. Ask students to choose their favorite physical characteristics by circling them on the Design a Pet graphic organizer (see page 99). Then, ask students to draw their newly designed pet using the various characteristics that they have selected. Finally, invite students to create a name for their type of pet, and display student creations on a bulletin board.

"Perfect Pets"

Sing this song to the tune of "Jingle Bells." After students have learned these verses, ask them to join you in creating additional verses to the song.

Perfect pets

Perfect pets

Perfect pets for us.

Oh what fun it is to play

With perfect pets all day.

Run around

Swim around

Gallop all day long

Oh what fun it is to play

With perfect pets all day!

The Practically Perfect Pajamas

by Erik Brooks. Winslow, 2000.

Percy, the big white polar bear, loves his red-footed pajamas with the gold trim more than anything else in the world. Unfortunately, the other polar bears tease him endlessly for being different. Finally, Percy bows to pressure and packs up his pajamas forever. Unfortunately, his decision proves disastrous as he encounters the hardships of life without pajamas—and the other bears still consider him a target. In the end, Percy and Aurora fox hatch the best plan of all.

Pajama Day

Invite students to wear their favorite cozy pajamas on the day that you read this story (or on the next day). Ask each student to be prepared to explain, in detail, why his or her pajamas are perfect. Would they be equally perfect for Percy, if they were available in his size?

If there is enough time available in your schedule, you will certainly want to host a pajama parade through the halls of the school with your pajama-clad class!

Perfect Pajama Design

Inform students that Percy's lovely red pajamas with the gold trim have, at last, worn out. Invite them to design a new pair of perfect pajamas for Percy, using the Percy template on page 100. After the design activity is complete, offer students an opportunity to explain what makes their new pair of Percy pajamas perfect for him.

"Polka Dot Pajamas"

Share the call and response jazz poem "Polka Dot Pajamas" with the class. (Note: If you have time or a volunteer to do so, reproduce the poem on large chart paper.) You can find the poem reproduced and illustrated by Oxford University Press at fds.oup.com/www.oup.com/pdf/elt/catalogue/0-19-433721-9-b.pdf.

First, read the whole poem together. Then, practice the call and response. Read the first phrase and invite students to join in on echoing the response. Once the group is comfortable with this format, invite individual students to join you as you read the "call" lines.

Arctic Polar Bear

Begin by asking students to notice what they learned about Percy's arctic home by reading *The Practically Perfect Pajamas*. Make a list of the things they learned. Now, combine your reading of The Practically Perfect Pajamas, featuring Percy the Polar Bear, with another arctic book:

📖 **Book Pairing:** *Polar Bear, Arctic Hare* by Eileen Spinelli, illustrated by Eugenie Fernandes. Wordsong, 2007.

After reading the poems in *Polar Bear, Arctic Hare*, generate a second list of the features and animals of the Arctic.

Poodlena

by E. B. McHenry. Bloomsbury Publishing, 2004.

Poodlena Pompadour is a pink, fluffy poodle living in a high-rise apartment building with her doting owner. She spends her days with her coiffeur, receiving hair and spa treatments and generally "pinking" up. In the late afternoons, after a day of primping, Poodlena finally deigns to be leashed and led to the park, where she sniffs at the playful dog packs, wanting only to be "seen." But on the day that Poodlena is accidentally knocked off her feet into a moat of mud, she discovers a whole new world of authentic fun.

Poodlena in Pink

Discuss the reasons that Poodlena looks so special. What do she and her master do that makes her exceptionally pretty to look at? Make a list of her physical characteristics and the primping that make her so perfect. Now, have students come up to the list and circle any items that begin with P, using a purple or pink marker, of course.

Perfectly Pink and Puffy Poodles

After reading the story, share pictures of poodles, noting what they have in common (fluffy fur). Discuss the similarities and differences between real-life poodles and Poodlena. Then, invite students to make their own fluffy, pink, puffy poodle.

Distribute the following materials to each student: one large pre-cut pink construction paper circle (poodle face), two pre-cut pink construction paper ovals (poodle ears), three pre-cut black construction paper circles (poodle eyes and nose), glue stick, nine pink cotton balls.

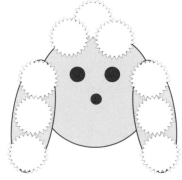

Ask students to follow your lead in creating their poodles by attaching one shape at a time to the large pink poodle face and end by attaching the three pink cotton balls to each ear and three pink cotton balls on the head for a fluff of hair.

Pretty Pooches

Poodle is one breed of dog that starts with P. Begin a discussion by brainstorming a list of other breeds that also begin with P, such as the Pug, Papillon, Pekingese, and so on. Then, ask students to gather in small groups, and instruct them to use dog breed books to find other breeds that begin with the letter P. Reassure them that it is okay if they cannot read the text of the books you supply. Explain how to look for a P at the beginning of the header for each

breed. Give each group a stack of pink post-it notes to apply to any page they think contains a P breed.

Now, visit the Dog Breed Info Center Web site at www.dogbreedinfo.com/abc.htm#P-Q, and share pictures of other P breeds of dogs. Discuss breeds that students found in the books and the breeds on the site, looking for another breed of dog that might be groomed to be as pink, pretty, and puffy as Poodlena.

"I Had a Poodle"

Teach your students the "I Had a Poodle" finger play poodle poem available at the CanTeach Web site at www.canteach.ca/elementary/songspoems47.html. To customize the rhyme to match Poodlena, consider changing the second line to "her coat was fluffy pink" and the gender throughout to female.

Piglet and Papa

by Margaret Wild, illustrated by Stephen Michael King. Abrams, 2007.

Piglet and her Papa are the best of friends and playmates until one day, Piglet is a little too rough and Papa chases her out of the sty. Worried and insecure, Piglet visits each of her other barnyard friends in turn, asking if they love her. Each time, she is reassured that they do love her, but that there is someone who loves her much, much more. Of course, that someone turns out to be Papa!

What Do You Call Your Papa?

Piglet calls her father Papa. Begin a discussion with your students by asking them to list all of the names they know for father or grandfather. (Note: In many Franco-American families, "Papa" is the name for Grandfather.) How many of the names begin with P? Ask students why they think that author Margaret Wild chose Papa for Piglet's father's name. When someone mentions the alliterative Ps, introduce the next step of this activity. For each other name for father or grandfather, ask them to come up with an alliterative title by changing the animal in the story. For instance, Gosling and Grandpa, Frog and Father, Pigeon and Pa, etc.

Piglet's Many P's?

Begin this vocabulary game with the following sentence:

Piglet is a **pig** whose father's name is **Papa**.

Write each word on a separate 3x5" sticky note, and attach them to the board or to a large chart. Now challenge students, one at a time, to add a word or phrase to the basic sentence that includes the letter P. For instance:

Piglet is a **pink pig** whose father's name is **Papa**.

Each time, write the new word or phrase on a sticky note and add it to the sentence. Invite the whole class to recite the new sentence along with you after each addition.

Piglet Math

Ask students to recall the progression of the story's barnyard characters, what these animals like about Piglet, and their numerical responses to Piglet during each encounter. Reproduce and fill in the Piglet Math chart with the class.

Barnyard Animal	What he/she likes about Piglet	Someone loves her x times more

Piglet Parts

Each barnyard animal that Piglet consults has a favorite part of Piglet—one of her piglet parts!

Invite students to "build a Piglet" by providing them with a pink piglet body, minus her parts. (Note: You can either cut the needed Piglets out of construction paper for gluing, or photocopy her onto white paper.) Use the Piglet Parts template on page 101.

Then, invite students to add her favorite parts, using their own artistic talents:

- cute little ears
- snub little nose
- curly-whirly tail
- little pink trotters
- fat little tummy

Design a Pet

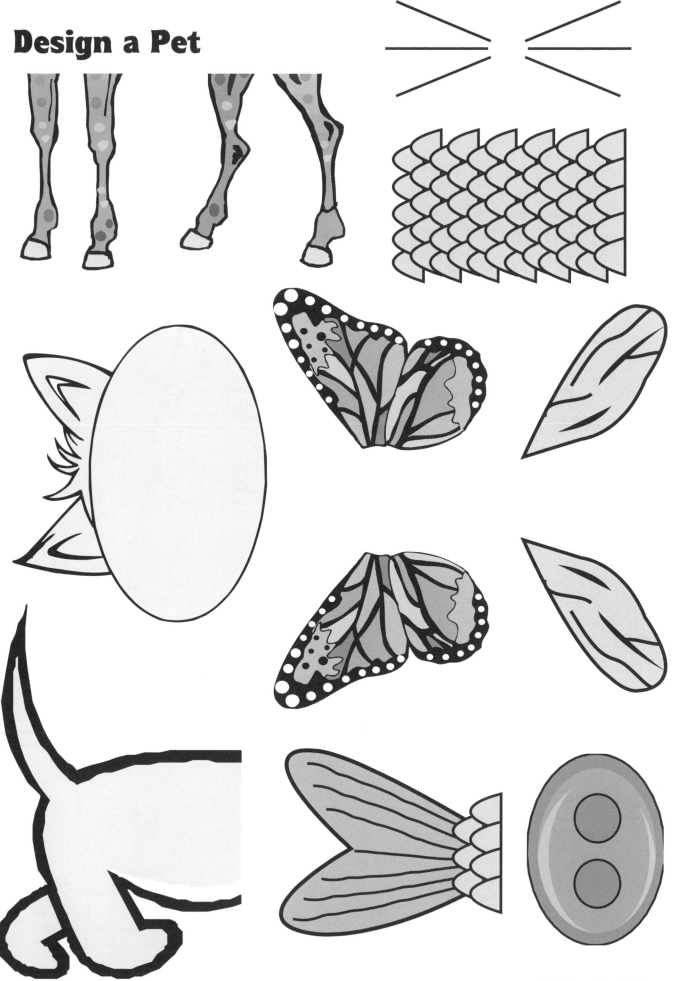

Perfect Pajama Design

The Name Quilt

by Phyllis Root, illustrated by Margot Apple. Farrar, Straus and Giroux, 2003.

At Grandma's house in summer, Sadie loves to be tucked in under the name quilt because Grandma tells exciting stories about the adventures of the people whose names are embroidered on the quilt's squares. As Grandma moves from square to square, Sadie's family history unfolds. One day, while Sadie and Grandma are out fishing, a violent summer storm blows the quilt away. Grandma remembers all of the names and stories, and Sadie and Grandma create a new quilt, with Sadie's name right in the center.

A Class Name Quilt

Make a list of the students in the class and a corresponding grid of the appropriate number of squares. (Note: if you have extra blank squares, you might consider adding class pets or important people in the school, such as the principal.) Use a lottery system to decide where each name will go on the quilt, and write the names in the template squares.

Next, determine whether this will be a paper quilt made from manila construction paper, or, if there is a parent in the class who is willing to assist with sewing, fabric. Either way, ask each student to create a scene with crayons (iron-transfer fabric crayons if it will be a fabric quilt) of an exciting or adventurous time in his or her life using the template below. (Note: If you are planning a fabric quilt, cut paper one half inch bigger than the center diamond of the template, and clearly mark one of the

"peaks" as the top.) Be sure each student's name is in his or her square.

Once the squares are taped together or displayed side by side on the wall or bulletin board (or sewn together), spend time asking each child to tell the story of the time depicted in his or her square.

A Family Name Quilt

Encourage students to work with an adult in their family to create a small (four-, six-, or nine-patch) quilt of family stories. Send home the directions, adapted from A Class Name Quilt (above), for making a paper quilt on manila construction paper. When students return to school with their family name quilts, allow each student to choose a name on the family quilt of the day and tell that person's story, just as Grandma does for Sadie.

Arrange a Quilt

Give each student a piece of white paper divided into nine equal squares, and nine equal-sized squares of colored construction paper or oaktag to match the size of the "quilt squares." Ask students to arrange the squares in as many different patterns as they can come up with. Each time someone creates a new pattern, reproduce it on an easel and ask all students to try it. Depending on developmental level of the students, you may want to proceed to the next level, which is to cut each of the nine quilt squares in half, diagonally, giving students eighteen triangles of three colors. Repeat the invitation to create new and different patterns with these.

"The Quilt Song"

Visit the Utah Education Network Web site to download a .pdf file of "The Quilt Song" at www.uen.org/Lessonplan/preview.cgi?LPid=18816. Sing the song to the tune of "I Have a Little Frog" (otherwise titled "Miss Suzy Had a Baby"). Talk about how the words of the song reflect the story in *The Name Quilt*, and the meaning of that quilt in Sadie's family.

The Recess Queen

by Alexis O'Neill, illustrated by Laura Huliska-Beith. Scholastic, 2002.

Until Katie Sue came to school, Mean Jean was the Recess Queen. She was the first to swing, the first to kick, the first to bounce, or there was a price to pay. However, teeny-tiny, open-hearted Katie Sue doesn't know the rules. When Mean Jean tries to set the record straight, Katie Sue talks back—and then invites Jean to jump with her—and Jean does, no longer mean.

What Makes a Queen a Queen?

Mean Jean is the Recess Queen at her school. Ask students about the behaviors that make her the queen. What does she DO as Recess Queen? What does she SAY? Do students agree, though, that she SHOULD be Queen? Once you have discussed Mean Jean's behavior, ask students to complete this sentence in as many ways as possible:

Mean Jean is Recess Queen because she

_____

but Katie Sue SHOULD be Recess Queen because she _____.

Two Queens

After reading *The Recess Queen*, read another picture book about bullying:

📖 **Book Pairing:** *Bootsie Barker Bites* by Barbara Bottner. Putnam, 1992.

If Mean Jean is the Recess Queen, then Bootsie Barker is the Play Date Queen. Invite students to discuss and compare the two characters. Use a text-to-text Venn Diagram to record the answers. Discussion questions might include:

- How does Jean bully?
- How does Bootsie bully?
- What would Jean do in *Bootsie Barker Bites*?
- What would Katie Sue do?
- What would Bootsie do in *The Recess Queen*?
- What would the *Bootsie Barker Bites* narrator do?

Jump Rope Queen

Katie Sue is certainly the queen of jump rope at her new school. She has the wonderful ability to make up rhythmic jump rope rhymes on the spot in order to invite Mean Jean to jump with her. Tell students that they will be writing a jump rope rhyme about Katie Sue. Before they do, invite them to listen to selected jump rope rhymes in the following book:

📖 **Book Pairing:** *Over in the Pink House: New Jump Rope Rhymes* by Rebecca KaiDotlich, illustrated by Melanie W. Hall. Boyds Mills Press, 2004.

Then ask students to create a Katie Sue jump rope rhyme of their own. For example:

> Katie Sue jumps.
>
> Katie Sue smiles.
>
> Mean Jean hears her
>
> across the miles.
>
> Katie Sue coaxes.
>
> Katie Sue smiles.
>
> Jean comes running
>
> across those miles.

Katie Sue jumps

with Mean Jean

Katie Sue is our

Jump Rope Queen.

Recess Queen or King

Ask students to think about your school's playground. If they were Recess Queens (or Kings) for the day, what especially nice things might they do while they were wearing the crown? You may want to fashion a gold crown like Mean Jean wears on the cover of *The Recess Queen* and allow students to take turns wearing it on the playground as they act out their ideas for being the nicest kind of royalty.

Little Quack

by Lauren Thompson, illustrated by Derek Anderson. Simon & Schuster, 2003. Scholastic, 2002.

Mama Duck tries to coax her five, fearful little ducklings out of the safe nest and into the water, but they are too scared. Finally, one at a time, four of them find the courage to plop into the pond in response to Mama's gentle encouragement. But Little Quack, the smallest duck, remains behind until he discovers that he can be brave, too.

What's in a Name?

Mama has five ducklings (Widdle, Waddle, Piddle, Puddle, and Little Quack). Write them on the board or on a chart, and ask students to remember their names. Now ask students a series of questions:

- Which name is the funniest?

- Which names rhyme with each other?

- Which name is two words long?

- Which character's name fits him or her best?

Ask students to explain their reasons for each of their answers.

A Duck by any Other Name

Mama Duck is not the only duck parent to have given her ducklings a series of unusual names. Mr. and Mrs. Mallard do, too in the most famous children's duck story of all:

📖 **Book Pairing:** *Make Way for Ducklings* by Robert McCloskey. Viking, 1941.

Invite students to recall the ducklings in this story (Jack, Kack, Lack, Mack, Nack, Ouack, Pack, and Quack). Ask some of the same questions that you asked in the What's in a Name? activity above. Then, ask the students what special pattern they notice in these eight names. Be sure that the students notice that the names rhyme, are in alphabetical order, and each feature a single syllable, and also that the list ends with the name that stands for the sound that ducks make.

Little Quick

Ask students to imagine that Mama Duck had six ducklings instead of five. The last duckling might have been named Little Quick. What would that name tell us about the sixth duckling? How would he behave? How would he fit into the *Little Quack* story? Challenge students to retell the story with this sixth duckling included. Then ask each student to draw a picture of Little Quick.

"Little Quack"

(Sing to the tune of "Jingle Bells.")

Quacking from the nest,
we follow Mama Duck.
Into the waves we go,
We all have good luck.

Widdle splishes in.
Waddle follows—SPLASH!
Piddle splooshes next.
Puddle sploshes last.

But where is Little Quack?
Are you still inside the nest?
Come and join us now!
Just try to do your best.

Oh, Little Quack! Little Quack!
Plunge into the pond.
Oh what fun it is to swing
with Little Quack along.

Little Quack! Little Quack!
You can do it too.
We all tried our best to swim
And now it's time for you.

A Class Name Quilt

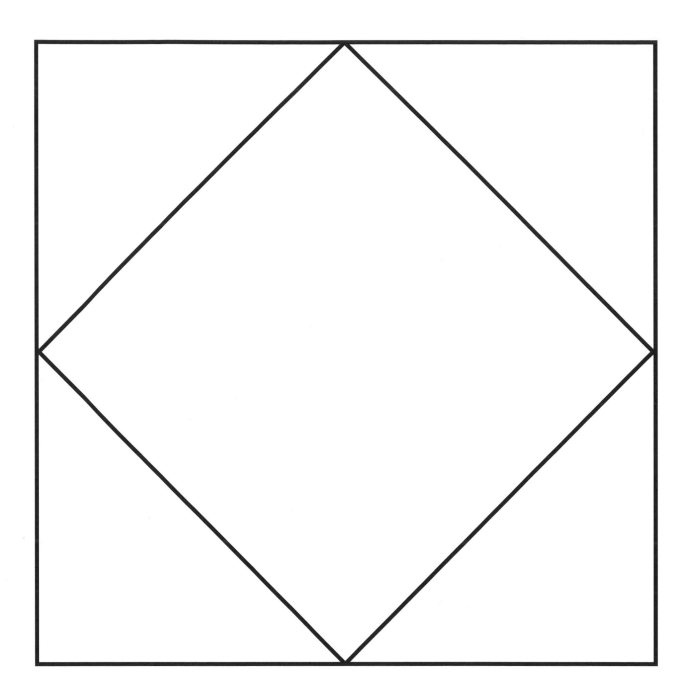

Red Red Red

**by Valeri Gorbachev.
Philomel Books, 2007.**

One summer evening when Turtle is rushing through town, he passes each of his animal neighbors (who are each actively involved with something bright red). He tells them, without stopping, that he is "off to see something red, red, red." Each neighbor wonders whether it isn't the very thing he or she is tending, but Turtle always says no. Each neighbor hops in line behind him to finally climb a hill to the lake and Turtle introduces them to the beautiful red sunset.

A Town Full of Red

The characters in *Red Red Red* join Turtle on his journey to something red. But all of them are busy with something red, themselves, when he comes by. Begin by re-reading the story and listing all of the red things that the animal neighbors are involved with. Reproduce this chart on your easel:

Neighbor	Red Object(s)

Then, ask students to add to the chart by naming people in your own town who work with or tend red items. Name these red items. (Note: Pairs might include a crossing guard holding a stop sign, an apple orchard owner, a gardener planting red tulips, a fireman driving

a fire engine, etc.) If you are in a neighborhood school, you may even want to take a walk around the neighborhood or downtown to complete this activity.

We're Going on a Red Hunt

Ask students to look around the library or classroom in which they are gathered for objects that are red, including the clothing they are wearing. Make a list of them.

Next, go on a walk throughout the school and hunt for things that are red. Take a clipboard and pen with you so that you can record each red item that they spot. Upon your return, add these items to the list of red objects that you originally compiled.

If time allows, ask students to go on a red hunt at home and make a list of the red objects they find there. The next time you gather, add these items to the list of red objects, too.

Finally, evaluate each found object by asking, "Can this come in another color besides red?" For those items on the list that can only be red, circle them with a red marker.

Exploring Cumulative Tales

Introduce your students to the concept of cumulative tales so that they understand that *Red Red Red* is one such story. To reinforce the concept, share the story of "Chicken Licken" with them. You can find the text of the story at the Ongoing Tales for the Family Web site at www.ongoing-tales.com/SERIALS/oldtime/ FAIRYTALES/chicklicken.html.

Or, you may choose to share a picture book version of the traditional "Henny Penny" story.

📖 **Book Pairing:** *Henny Penny* by Vivian French, illustrated by Sophie Windham. Bloomsbury Publishing, 2007.

Henny Penny by Paul Galdone. Clarion Books, 1979.

Ask students to discuss the ways that "Chicken Licken" or *Henny Penny* "work" in the same way that *Red Red Red* does. What are the similarities?

Red Red Red Retelling

Using the templates on pages 111–112, make a set of the characters mounted on popsicle sticks or using the flannel board. Ask students to retell the story using these props.

Rhinos Who Rescue

**by Julie Mammano.
Chronicle Books, 2007.**

The crew members in this story are rhino firefighters, ready to tackle any job, no matter how big—or small. They jump on their big rig each time and rush to the rescue, whether they are headed to a big blaze, a gnarly pileup, or a small, stranded kitten. These heroes are brave and dedicated no matter what the emergency is. Written with firefighter lingo throughout (and a glossary to explain it all), *Rhinos Who Rescue* is a child-friendly picture book.

Rescuers

Ask students to define the word "rescue." Write down their answers to the question: "What does it mean to rescue something or someone?" Once you have exhausted student contributions, refer to a primary dictionary such as *Merriam-Webster's Primary Dictionary* by Ruth Heller (2005). If students are familiar with the use of a dictionary, ask them where they think "rescue" will be found. Share the dictionary definition.

Now ask them to name other people in the community, in addition to firefighters, who might be considered rescuers. Then invite students to share stories of times when they were rescued or had an encounter with a rescuer. Discuss their experiences.

Rescue Rig

When the rhino firefighters are called, "They jump on their rig and bolt to the blaze." Show students that the word "rig" is defined in the glossary as a fire truck or fire engine. As students examine the illustrations in *Rhinos Who Rescue*, ask them to tell you everything they notice about the fire truck pictured. What are its features and how are they used? Then share this nonfiction book about all of the components of fire trucks to learn more:

📖 **Book Pairing:** *Fire Truck Factory* by Catherine Anderson. Heinemann Library, 2005.

Rescuers in Your Town

If possible, schedule a field trip to the fire station to extend students' learning. If this is not possible, invite a firefighter to come to your school to talk to students. Prepare questions ahead of time by taking note of the questions that students ask about both rescuers and rigs as you read and extend *Rhinos Who Rescue*.

African Rhinos

Of course, real rhinoceroses do not ride in fire trucks or rescue people. Instead, they live in parts of Africa and Asia where they need to be rescued because they are endangered. Read more about the species of rhinos still in existence in books such as:

📖 **Book Pairing:** *Black Rhino* by Louise and Richard Spilsbury. Heinemann, 2006.

Rhinos: Horn-Faced Chargers by Lola M. Schaefer. Bridgestone Books, 2002.

You and the class may choose to help save the severely endangered Sumatran rhino. If so, visit the International Rhino Federation Web site at www.rhinos-irf.org/adoptarhino.

To learn about the extinct wooly rhinoceros visit another page of the site at www.rhinos-irf.org/woolly.

Rainy Day Fun

After reading *Red Rubber Boot Day,* ask students to join you in making a list of all of the things that the main character loves to do on a rainy day. List them down the Y-axis of a matrix and then invite students to indicate which is their favorite rainy day activity out of those featured in the book. Use the matrix results as the basis for a math discussion as the graph takes shape.

Next, invite students to add to the list of activities that they personally enjoy on rainy days that are not mentioned in the book. Then, repeat the graphing activity with a new matrix, and ask students to interpret the results on this new graph.

Rainy Day Reading

Host a rainy day read-in! Choose a rainy day for this activity or, if it is sunny outside, simply pretend that it is raining! (Note: You may want to pull the shades, if so.) Now, invite each student to choose a book or two that they have been wanting to spend time with, and instruct them to find a place to create a "reading cave." If you don't have a coat closet, consider bringing in sheets so that students can make under-desk or under-table caves. Then, play a CD with rain (and possibly thunder) sounds if you want to add to the drama that nature provides.

Red Rubber Boots

"Red rubber made-for-rain boots" are what the narrator loves for puddle splashing on a rainy day. Ask each student to draw a large picture of themselves outside on a rainy day in bare feet like Mr. Humphrey. Then, using red construction paper, a marker, scissors, and a glue stick, invite each student to design a pair of red rubber boots that they glue onto the figure in their painting.

"It's Raining, It's Pouring"

Sing the classic children's song, "It's Raining, It's Pouring" with the class. Find the words and music to the song at the National Institutes of Health, Department of Health & Human Services Web site at <u>kids.niehs.nih.gov/lyrics/ itsraining.htm</u>.

Once they are familiar with the song, challenge them to write a second verse as a class. Using a written copy of the poem on the board or a chart, explain the rhyme pattern of the original song to students:

A

A

B

B

A

The initial challenge will be to come up with an easily rhymed word for the end of the first line, as you will want two other useful words to rhyme with it in the second and last lines!

Rainy Day Pairing

Read *Red Rubber Boot Day* along with *Rain Romp: Stomping Away a Grouchy Day*. Now, begin by exploring the ways the two narrators experience a rainy day. The rain makes each of them feel very differently, except for the intersection when they are out romping, stomping, and splashing in the rain. Because of this, the two companion books lend themselves to a Venn diagram comparison. Allow discussion to unfold for awhile before introducing the Venn diagram graphic organizer for their thoughts.

> ### Rain Romp: Stomping Away a Grouchy Day
>
> **by Jane Kurtz, illustrated by Dyanna Wolcott. Greenwillow Books, 2002.**
>
> The young narrator of this picture book wakes up to a "gray, grouchy day." Furthermore, the sky agrees with her! Despite crooning and coaxing from two generous parents, she can't let go of her feelings of gloom until she stomps out into the rain and does a "Raaaaaain romp!" with her parents.

Rain Romping Reader's Theater

After you have read aloud *Rain Romp: Stomping Away a Grouchy Day* a few times, create a bit of reader's theater with your class. First, choose some of the easier-to-read/remember lines and write them out on sentence strips. Give these strips to some of your eager readers. Then, teach everyone else (the chorus) this chant: "Rain romp! Rain stomp! Rain rain romp and stomp!" Act as narrator yourself, and let your readers know when it is their turn to read their lines. Periodically, point to your chorus to perform their chant.

If you have a group of reading buddies or older students to pair with your class, you might want them to present the full *Rain Romp: Stomping Away a Grouchy Day* reader's theater as published in the March 2006 issue of *LibrarySparks Magazine.*

And the Rain Comes Down

With your students, create an enormous rain cloud either from gray or black craft paper, or by painting one on white craft paper. (Note: Make the rain cloud three dimensional by cutting two cloud shapes of the same size, stuffing them with newspaper, and stapling the edges.) Mount the rain cloud on the wall and then invite students to create a rain storm by taping up silver holiday tinsel at a slanting angle.

"Little Black Rain Cloud"

Once your rain cloud from the activity above is complete, teach your students to sing "Little Black Rain Cloud." Find lyrics and an abbreviated music clip at the National Institutes of Health, Department of Health & Human Services Web site at kids.niehs.nih.gov/lyrics/raincloud.htm.

Red Red Red Retelling

Red Red Red Retelling

Sleep, Black Bear, Sleep

by Jane Yolen and Heidi E. Y. Stemple, illustrated by Brooke Dyer. HarperCollins, 2007.

In this lovely, rhyming ode to hibernation and sleep, Yolen presents the hibernation habits of 12 animals. Illustration and text offer lots of information about when, where, and how the animals spend their winters, and soft cozy illustrations also reinforce and extend concepts—while also adding a good dose of humor. This lullaby poem ends with a child sleeping "through winter or through summer storm" under a quilt to keep her warm.

Hibernation Is a Long Sleep

The animals in *Sleep, Black Bear, Sleep* hibernate all winter. After reading the book to the class, ask students what they know about hibernation. Discuss ways that hibernation is similar to our sleep, and how it is different. Consider reading another hibernation picture book before you begin the discussion to broaden student understanding of the concept:

📖 **Book Pairing:** *Time to Sleep* by Denise Fleming. Henry Holt, 1997.

Now, use a Venn diagram to compare the hibernation habits of various animals to each other and to human sleep.

Sleep by Any Other Name

Begin by discussing synonyms (another S word!). Practice thinking of synonyms for common words such as hot and cold. Now, ask the class to have their detective hats on tight, and reread the book. When you finish, ask students to try to list all the words that the author uses for sleep in the poem.

Who Sleeps Where?

The animals in *Sleep, Black Bear, Sleep* hibernate all winter, but they each do so in many different places and in many different ways. On a large, four-column chart formatted like the sample below, list the 12 animals that hibernate in the book. Ask students to draw a picture of one of the animals of their choice hibernating, and have them cut it out. Now, instruct students to glue their animal next to its name on the list. Finish the chart by completing the two additional columns.

Animal	Pictures	Where It Sleeps	How It Sleeps

Extension: Create a display of photographs of the students snuggled down in their own beds.

Sing a Hibernation Song

Several clever educators have created hibernation songs to familiar children's songs. Visit The Perpetual Preschool Web site at www.perpetualpreschool.com/preschool_themes/hibernation/hibernation_songs.htm where you will also find links to hibernation art activities and games.

Slippers at School

by Andrew Clements, illustrated by Janie Bynum. Dutton, 2005.

Slippers the dog knows something is afoot the morning he wakes up to find Laura getting ready for the first day of school. He slips into Laura's open backpack. All day long, Slippers explores the school, from the classroom, to the kitchen, to the gym, to the principal's office. He is spotted, but never captured. Before the day is over, he slips back into Laura's backpack and returns home, leaving Laura none the wiser and wishing she could take Slippers to school someday.

A Perfect Name

Discuss the source of Slippers' name with the class. Invite students to draw a picture of their favorite pet, real or imagined. Now, ask them to draw slippers on the pet. If you would like to add a focus on colors to the activity, ask them to give the pet one red slipper and one blue slipper (for two-footed animals) and an additional green slipper and orange slipper for four-footed animals.

Little Dog Lost

Slippers explores all over Laura's school. With the class, make a list of the places he slips off to, starting in Laura's classroom. Now invite students to create a class map of your school, labeling it in large letters with the school's name. If you have room, use chart paper to make the map very large and post it on a wall or in the hallway. Draw and label the places that Slippers might visit.

Find the page that shows Slippers running around a corner, and photocopy and laminate it. Attach a piece of wide, strong roller tape to the back side. Then, give each student a turn to move Slippers to a new spot, asking them to say, aloud, "Slippers slips to _____ in _____ School.

Slipper Day

Host a slipper day in the library or the classroom, or take Slipper Day school-wide! Ask each student to bring in his or her slippers to wear all day. (You may want to have a small collection of extra slippers for those who forget.) Chart the slippers in the class in a variety of ways: by color, by style, etc. Then hold a contest in which you vote on the slippers in a variety of categories and award certificates. Create enough categories so that every student gets a certificate (see page 117). Categories might include: funniest, furriest, most colorful, scariest, warmest, etc.

Sing a Song of School

A wonderful collection of songs and poems about school can be found on the CanTeach Web site at www.canteach.ca/elementary/songspoems5.html.

Some Smug Slug

by Pamela Duncan Edwards, illustrated by Henry Cole. HarperCollins, 1996.

Slug is on a journey as the story begins. With his little eyes up on their stalks on a summery Sunday, he is taking a stroll across the soil when he suddenly senses a slope. He starts up, despite the screams of the sparrow, the shrieks of the spider, the snickers of the skink, the scolding of the squirrel, or the comments of the stinkbug and the swallowtail. He is a self-satisfied slug, smiling all the way up to the toad's waiting mouth.

Find an S

Illustrator Herbert Cole painted an "S" shape in every picture in this book. Challenge students to find the S in each picture.

Sparkling Scribble

Begin by discussing how slugs move along a slippery path they create. Give each student a copy of the graphic organizer with Smug Slug in the corner (see page 118). Ask them to color the slug and then draw in his surroundings. Now ask them to choose a special color of crayon to draw the scribble path he has been on. After each child has drawn Smug Slug's scribble path, let him or her trace over it with a Glitter Glue pen.

Can You Stroll, Signal, and Scurry?

Smug Slug and the other animals move in a variety of ways that begin with S. Introduce the meaning of each action and then ask your students to practice moving in these ways:

- stroll (slug)
- signal (slug, with antennae)
- scurry (spider)
- swoosh (swallowtail)
- swish (skink, with tail)
- shrug (slug, with shoulders)
- swagger (slug)
- slither (slug)
- shiver (stinkbug)
- slumber (slug)
- swerve (slug)
- straggle (slug)
- sway (slug)
- skew (slug)
- shamble (slug)
- struggle (slug)
- shift (toad)
- shudder (toad)
- shake (toad)

Animals that Begin with S

Slug isn't the only S animal in this story. In fact, every animal that warns Slug or worries about him also starts with the letter S, including:

- sparrow
- spider
- swallowtail
- skink
- squirrel
- stinkbug

In addition, the illustrations include these additional S animals:

- skunk
- snake
- salamander
- snails

Invite students to add other S animals to the list that are not included in the story. Use an assortment of books to explore these other S animals and learn more about them.

Extension: Ask students to divide the entire list of S animals into animal groups. Use formal classifications (i.e., birds, mammals, fish, etc.) if these are familiar to your students, or use a simpler system, such as fur, feathers, scales, etc.

Snip, Snip . . . Snow!

by Nancy Poydar. Holiday House, 1997.

As winter arrives with cold days requiring jackets and mittens and hoods, Sophie is disappointed because there is no snow. When a big storm is predicted, her excitement rises and her hopes soar, but the storm stalls. In an attempt to overcome her disappointment, Sophie suggests that her class make their own snowflakes and hang them. As if by magic, the paper snow brings on the real thing—much to Sophie's delight.

All About Snow

Begin discussion of *Snip, Snip . . . Snow!* by talking about snow. What is it? What does it look like? What does it feel like? Then, share a nonfiction book about snow to build student background knowledge:

📖 **Book Pairing:** *Who Likes the Snow?* by Etta Kaner, illustrated by Marie Lafrance. Kids Can Press, 2006.

After reading *Who Likes the Snow?* ask students if they have more questions about snow. If they do, follow the format of the book and make a statement about snow. Follow it with a question. Then head to the library to do "snow research," and create an explanation that answers the question.

Handmade Snow

When the snowstorm fails to arrive, Sophie and her classmates make their own snowflakes. Have your students do the same. Provide them with precut circles of white paper or white coffee filters for large flakes. Then, follow the instructions on the last page of *Snip, Snip . . . Snow!* To make it easier for young hands, you may want to mark fold-and-cut lines. For the youngest students, providing an older student buddy will be helpful. Be prepared for a flurry of paper snow scraps with this activity!

Winter Starts with S

Many of the activities that Sophie wants to do when it snows start with S. Return to the text and ask students to find the activities that begin with S and list them on a chart (shoveling, make snowballs, make snowmen, go sledding). Now ask students to brainstorm more S activities related to snow (sliding, making snow angels, skating, skiing, etc.). When the list is complete, invite each student to select one activity and illustrate it. Label the picture with the S word it depicts.

Picture the Snow

Using a three-hole punch, create tiny snowflakes from white scrap paper. Fill a small paper cup halfway for each student. Supply each student with a sheet of black construction paper and a glue stick. Ask them to draw a snowy scene, one quadrant at a time, with the glue stick, and then sprinkle the snow over the glue. Allow backdrops to dry. Then, ask students to draw a picture of themselves dressed in winter coats, pants, boots, hats, mittens, and scarves on a smaller piece of white paper, and color it. After they have cut out their winter self-portrait, instruct them to glue it onto their snow scene.

Playing in the Snow

For a host of snowy indoor activities, including many reproducibles, visit the EdHelper.com Web site at edhelper.com/winter.htm.

Sing a Winter Song

Several clever educators have created winter songs set to the music of familiar children's songs. Visit The Perpetual Preschool Web site at www.perpetualpreschool.com/preschool themes/ice/ice_songs.htm where you will also find links to winter art activities and games.

Slipper Day

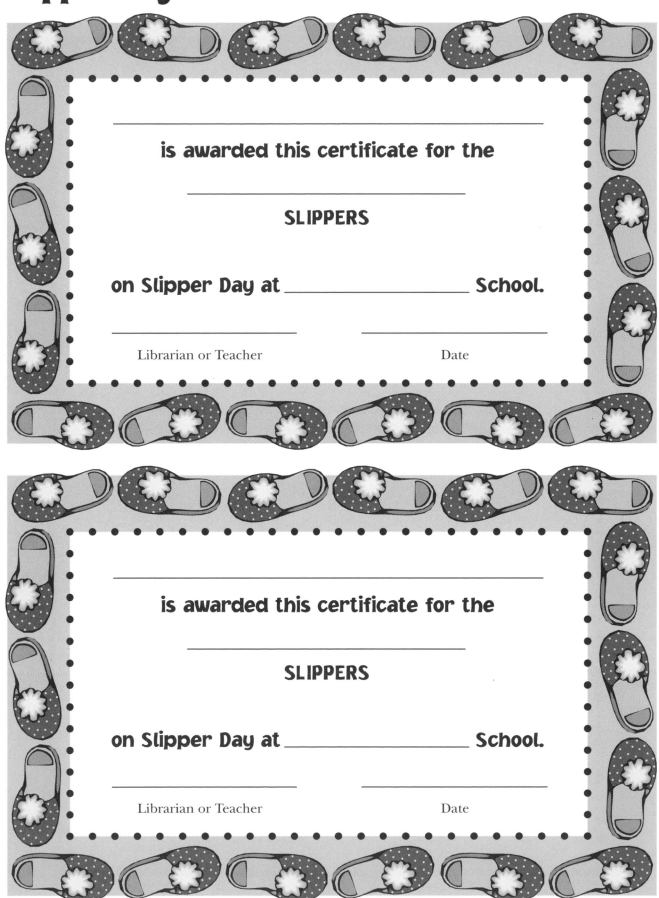

_____

is awarded this certificate for the

_____

SLIPPERS

on Slipper Day at _____ **School.**

_____   _____
Librarian or Teacher   Date

_____

is awarded this certificate for the

_____

SLIPPERS

on Slipper Day at _____ **School.**

_____   _____
Librarian or Teacher   Date

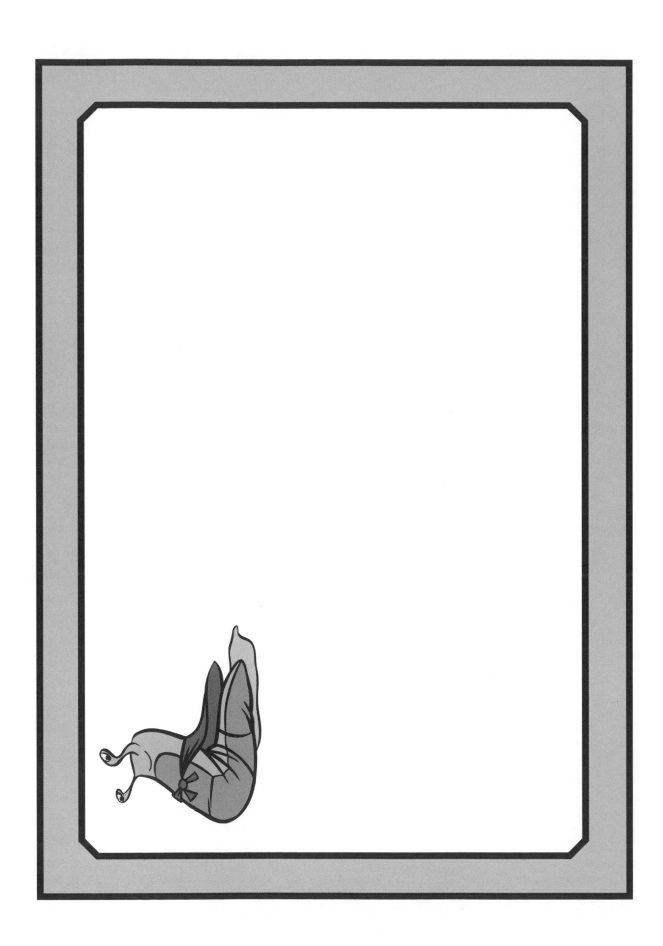

Sparkling Scribble

Mr. Tanen's Ties

by Maryann Cocca-Leffler. Albert Whitman, 1999.

Mr. Tanen, the crazy, tie-wearing principal of Lynnhurst Elementary School, has every kind of tie until the day that stuffy Mr. Apple at the School Department forbids him to wear anything but plain blue ties. Mr. Tanen sadly complies, and it is not until crabby Mr. Apple subs for Mr. Tanen that the true importance (and fun!) of the ties hits home—and even wins him a sweetheart. At last, Mr. Tanen returns to his crazy ties, and Mr. Apple joins him.

Mr. Tanen's Tie Closet

Invite students to bring in a collection of fun and interesting neckties for display. Attach a clothesline to a bulletin board titled MR. TANEN'S TIE CLOSET, and display the ties on the line. Ask each student to choose a tie, and have them discuss the type of school day on which Mr. Tanen would wear that tie. What would be the special person, event, weather, or mood that the tie would celebrate? Write student responses on colorful 3x5" index cards, and post them near the ties.

A Tie for Me

Mr. Tanen has all kinds of ties. Ask your students if they could have just ONE tie, what would it look like? Would the tie be a pattern or image of their favorite animal, their favorite sport, their favorite person, or their favorite place? Maybe it would have a little of each, or maybe it would just feature an interesting design, or the students' names.

Invite students to design their signature ties using the tie template on page 123. Attach elastic to each tie so students can wear them.

Ten Terrific Ties

Using the template on page 124, have a volunteer cut stacks of ties from colorful oaktag. Divide students into pairs and supply each pair with a stack of ten ties. Ask teams to divide the ties into two piles to represent all of the ways to add two numbers to equal ten. For example: one pile of one tie and one pile of nine ties equals TEN TIES. Ask students to write the equation $1 + 9 = 10$. Follow suit for the remaining eight equations.

Tie Tie-Ins

Author Maryann Cocca-Leffler has written two other stories about Mr. Tanen and his ties.

📖 **Book Pairing:** *Mr. Tanen's Tie Trouble* by Maryann Cocca-Leffler. Albert Whitman, 2003.

Mr. Tanen's Ties Rule! by Maryann Cocca-Leffler. Albert Whitman, 2003.

After sharing the two other Mr. Tanen stories with students, ask them to discuss the ways in which ties are the essential elements in each of the books. You may want to use a triple Venn diagram to explore similarities and differences.

Mr. Tanen Had a Tie

Remind students of the song "Old MacDonald Had a Farm," and then introduce the Mr. Tanen version. Ask them to join you and fill in the blanks as they go.

Mr. Tanen had a tie, E-I-E-I-O

And on his tie he had a/some _____, E-I-E-I-O

With a _____ _____ here and a _____ _____ there

Here a _____, there a _____, everywhere a _____ _____

Mr. Tanen had a tie, E-I-E-I-O

Supply the words by looking first at the ties in *Mr. Tanen's Ties*. Once you've exhausted the ties in the book, you'll have fun creating your own tie ideas for Mr. Tanen.

Trashy Town

by Andrea Zimmerman and David Clemensha, illustrated by Dan Yaccarino. HarperCollins, 1999.

Every morning, Mr. Gilly the trash man drives around looking for trash. Everywhere he goes, he dumps the trash, smashes it down, and drives on. The repeating refrain, "Is the trash truck full yet? NO. Mr. Gilly drives on" provides an opportunity for listeners to get in on the act until every bit of trash is deposited into the town dump. Then, Mr. Gilly turns his attention to cleaning himself up in the bath!

Town Trash

Begin by brainstorming all of the places that Mr. Gilly collects trash in Trashy Town. List them on a chart. For each one, mark whether you have a similar place in your town where trash could be collected. Now, ask students to brainstorm other places in your town where trash is collected, and add these places to the list. If time allows, ask students to draw a picture of Mr. Gilly collecting trash from one of those places in your town.

Trucking Along

Mr. Gilly drives a garbage truck in trashy town. But there are probably many other kinds of trucks in Trashy Town, too. Gather as many truck and vehicle books as possible from the nonfiction shelves in the library. Ask students to use these books to conduct truck research, and have them identify as many other types of trucks as possible.

When they are finished, direct students to draw a picture of one truck, color it, and cut it out.

Now, create a Trashy Town mural with Mr. Gilly's truck at the dump. Ask students to add a drawing on the mural of the place where their truck would appear, and then glue their truck picture on the mural with a glue stick.

Our Green Earth

Use a reading of *Trashy Town* to initiate a conversation about keeping the earth green. Mr. Gilly finds many trash cans full of trash to dump into his truck. However, it's possible that some of what is in those cans could be recycled instead.

Work with students to create a list of items that your town recycles, or that could be donated to Goodwill or another community source for used items. Ask them to share this list with their families. You might even want to keep an ongoing chart of how many recyclables were diverted from the trash in your own library or classroom.

Sing a Song of Trash

Introduce students to the song "Don't Dump Trash" which is recorded on *Environmental Songs for Kids* by Coco Kallis (Smithsonian Folkways Recordings - SFW45048, 1999). The song can also be individually purchased for download at the same site.

Clean Up with Good Books

If you find that your class is wild about trash and garbage trucks, continue the fun with another book about a garbage collection.

📖 **Book Pairing:** *I Stink!* by Kate McMullan, illustrated by Jim McMullan. HarperCollins, 2002.

Even young children will understand the concept of point of view when the two books are compared. After reading *I Stink!*, ask the students, "Who is talking?" Expect a lively conversation.

Trouble on the T-Ball Team

by Eve Bunting, illustrated by Irene Trivas. Clarion, 1997.

The ten-member Dodgers t-ball team keeps losing things! One at a time, the first-person narrator recounts the names of the players who have lost things, as well as the places and events surrounding the loss. All the while, the narrator feels worried. She's the only player who hasn't lost one. One what? She's not telling . . . until the day of the last game, when she is running so hard that she trips over the yellow dog that is running beside her. FINALLY, she loses one, too . . . her very first tooth!

What's It All About?

Some students will need an introduction to t-ball, and others will be players themselves and know a good deal about it.

You may want to do this activity before you read the book. Begin by explaining the basics of the game. If you need some background information, visit the T-Ball USA Association Web site at <www.teeballusa.org/Tball.asp>. Explain the rules of the game (click on the link at <www.teeballusa.org/Kids.asp>). If you have a very interested and experienced group, you may want to compare the rules of t-ball to those of baseball. Emphasize similarities and differences. Encourage students to begin their statements with the following language: "This rule is similar to/different from the rule for baseball because . . ."

Mapping the Field

There is a wonderful overhead illustration of the t-ball field in the middle of *Trouble on the T-Ball Team*. Enlarge this field map and display it after reading the story through once or twice. Give students paper and ask them to draw one of the ten players from the story. Remind them that every player but the narrator has a missing tooth. Assign someone to draw the yellow dog.

Now, using removable glue dots, ask students to re-enact the final scene when the narrator looses her tooth. Place emphasis on an accurate sequencing of events narrated in the book.

Tooth Game Time

Using your digital whiteboard or a computer with data projector hookup, visit the Colgate Kids World Web site and enjoy the offerings:

Colgate Kids World at <www.colgate.com/app/Kids-World/US/HomePage.cvsp>.

You may especially like to play "Lost Tooth Corner."

Save That Tooth!

Use the pattern on page 125 to cut two identical white fabric shapes out for each student (fleece or felt will work best). Attach a small colored fabric pocket to the front of one of the shapes.

Instruct students to use markers to decorate the front of one tooth shape with a face (consider supplying googly eyes if you have extra adult hands to help). Now use craft glue to attach the two shapes just along the outer edges, leaving an opening big enough for little fingers to stuff the pillow with batting once it is dry.

Provide polyester batting for stuffing the pillows and help students to glue the final opening shut.

Tooth Count Out!

Give each student a copy of the Tooth Count Out! graphic organizer on page 126 and ask them to compare the teeth they currently have in their mouths. For any missing teeth, ask them to place an X on the tooth. For any brand-new "adult" teeth, ask them to place a ✓.

Once students have completed their graphic organizers, you may wish to chart the number of baby teeth, missing teeth, loose teeth, and "adult" teeth in the class.

Sing a Loose Tooth Song

There are many poems and songs about loose teeth. Share some of them with your students. You'll find several at the "Teeth and Dental Health" page of the CanTeach Web site at www.canteach.ca/elementary/songspoems38.html.

Mr. Tuggle's Troubles

by LeeAnn Blankenship, illustrated by Karen Dugan. Boyds Mills Press, 2005.

Each day when Mr. Tuggle awakes in his disaster area of an apartment, he is missing a piece of clothing. He proceeds to the office regardless, but the missing piece of clothing always proves to be a necessity, and he must use his ingenuity to design a makeshift replacement. As days pass, he is soon decked out entirely in substitutes. When he catches sight of himself in a mirror, he determines to mend his ways by cleaning up his apartment and locating all of the missing items. . . . Or does he?

Tidy Is as Tidy Does

Begin by discussing Mr. Tuggle's problem. Ask students what his main trouble is. Once they have established that all of his troubles stem from his untidiness, discuss what it means to be tidy.

Ask students to study the first three pages of *Mr. Tuggle's Troubles*. What clues do they see that signal that Mr. Tuggle is untidy? Ask them

to complete the following statement each time they reply: "I know Mr. Tuggle is not tidy because . . ."

Tidy Up

Ask students to close their eyes and imagine their own bedroom or playroom at home. Take them through an imaginary trip into the room, starting at the door and scanning from left to right and from top to bottom. Have them stop when they see something out of place, and make a mental note of it. Then ask them to continue as you talk them around the room.

Once everyone has made a mental note of the objects out of place in their rooms, provide them with a piece of white paper with a dividing line down the center and the label UNTIDY on the left and TIDY on the right. Ask them to draw the item that is currently out of place where it is on the left and the item put away in its proper place on the right side.

Trouble Leads to Trouble

Mr. Tuggle's Troubles is a cumulative story with a repeating pattern. Each day, Mr. Tuggles repeats the previous day's events, but with a new item of clothing. Ask your students to determine the pattern, and then have them take turns reporting the new events following a consistent script.

On _____ morning, Mr. Tuggle couldn't find his _____.

He looked everywhere but he couldn't find his _____.

He decided he didn't need his _____.

So he went to work without it, but at the_____, he _____.

Back in his office, he made a _____ out of _____.

Later he wore his _____ home.

What Next?

Ask students to look at the illustration on the last page. Considering the pattern in the story, what do they predict will be Mr. Tuggle's next trouble? How might it continue?

A Tie for Me

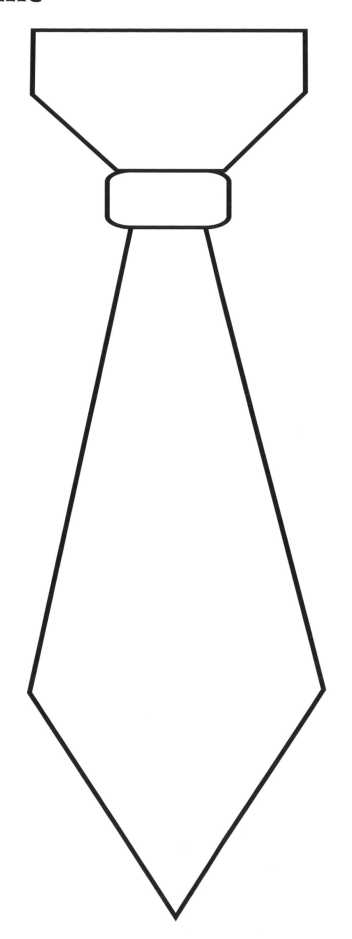

Ten Terrific Ties

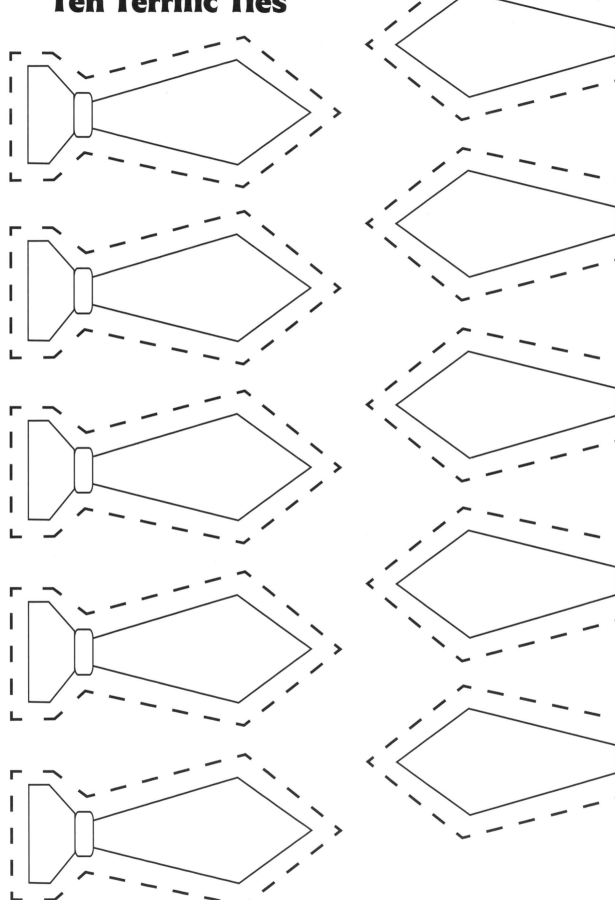

Save That Tooth!

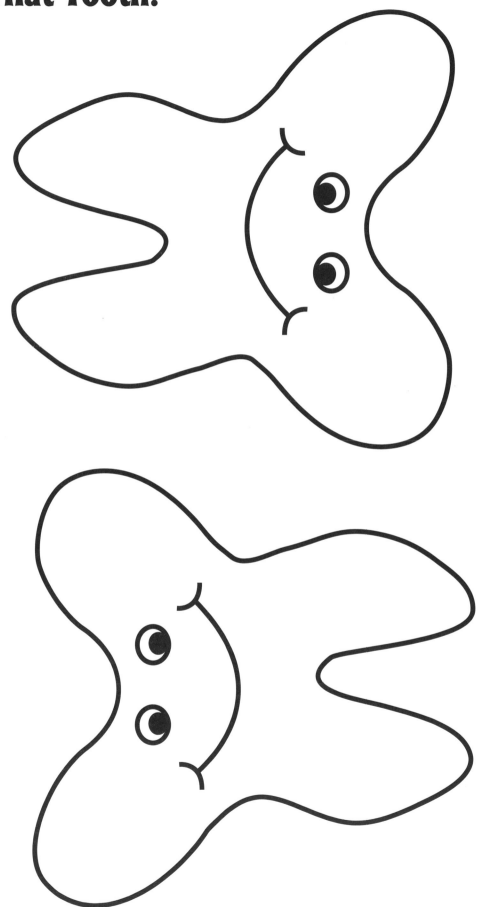

Tooth Count Out!

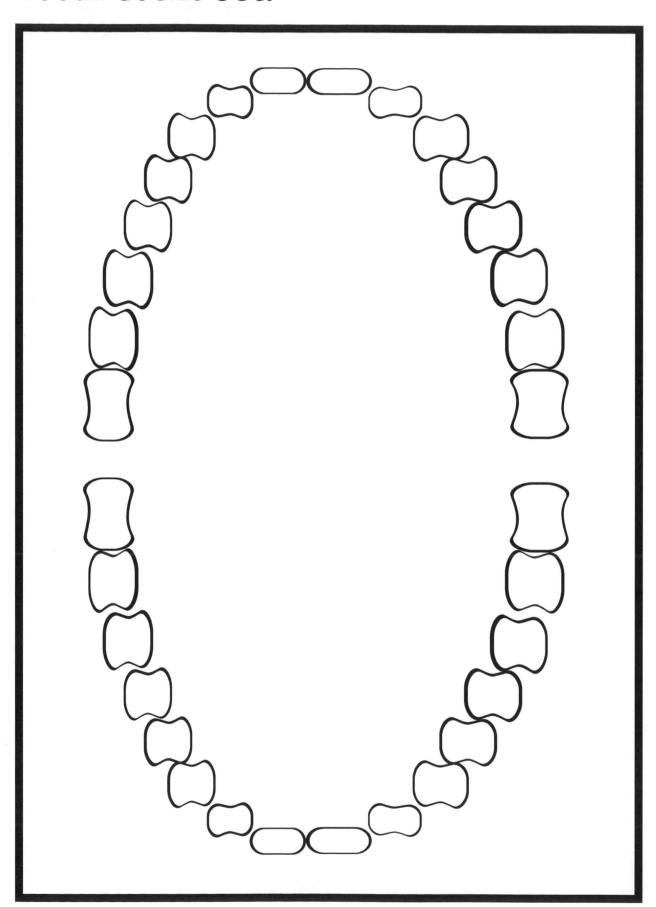

The Midnight Unicorn

by Neil Reed. Sterling, 2005.

Whenever Millie's dad asks her if there's anything special she'd like to do, Millie asks to go to the park to visit the small stone statue of a unicorn. Before long, the unicorn comes to life and Millie climbs astride with Casper, the family dog, bounding after them. They fly through the skies and traverse the globe, finally joining a herd of other unicorns. At last, the three adventurers fall asleep. When she awakens, Millie is back in the park with her father, an unexplained tropical flower tucked behind her ear.

Glue the Horn on the Unicorn

This activity is played much like Pin the Tail on the Donkey. Post a large drawing or poster of a unicorn on the wall. Create a set of Unicorn horns from the template on page 130. Hand out horns to each student to color, and write their names on the back. Then, using removable adhesive glue dots on the horns, blindfold students, give them a spin, and ask them to glue the horn on the unicorn. The student

who comes closest to the forehead with his or her horn has the privilege of borrowing your copy of *The Midnight Unicorn*.

Are Unicorns Real?

Discuss theories about unicorns with the class. Explain that for many years, scientists have been trying to determine which animal or animals might have given people ideas about unicorns. For your own background knowledge, read more at the Museum of Natural History Web site at www.amnh.org/exhibitions/mythic creatures/land/unicorns.php.

Since the most likely explanation for the rise of the unicorn myth is the narwhal, take some time to share photographs of narwhals (available online at the Narwhal.info Web site at www.narwhal.info/album/Photos and to discuss their similarities and differences from unicorns. You may want to create a Venn diagram for this purpose.

Underwear

by Mary Elise Monsell, illustrated by Lynn Munsinger. Albert Whitman, 1988.

Zachary Zebra and Orfo the Orangutan love underwear! In fact, every year they attend the World's Greatest Grassland Underwear Fair where they discover, buy, and wear new patterns, new styles, and new fabrics. But Bismark the Buffalo does NOT like underwear. He won't wear or even SAY underwear until Zachary and Orfo convince him. Then, Bismark discovers what all kids know—underwear is the funniest word in the English language. Luckily for Bismark, it cheers him up remarkably.

Underwear Word Play

With a focus on the letter U, invite students to brainstorm a list of U words. Once you have a long list, complete the following two sentences with some of those U words:

My underwear is _____

_____. (e.g., ugly, upside down)

My underwear has _____

_____ on it. (e.g., umbrellas, uncles)

My Favorite Pair

Ask students to go back to *Underwear* and pay special attention to all the different patterns on Zachary and Orfo's underwear. Invite them to talk about their own favorite pair of underwear and what pattern it has. Then, pass out the My Favorite Pair graphic organizer on page 131 and ask students to design their NEXT favorite pair of underwear.

Who Wears Underwear?

We see a lot of animals in underwear in *Underwear.* Invite the class to brainstorm an additional list of animals that do not appear in the book. Once the list is full of amazing choices, invite students to choose one animal and draw it in its underwear.

"Big Underwear" Song

Like Bismark the Buffalo, kids find the word "underwear" funnier than almost any other word. And it's all the more fun when they can sing it. For a fabulous school-friendly underwear song, you'll find the lyrics to "Big Underwear" by Joe Scrugs at the Songs for Teaching Web site at <u>www.songsforteaching.com/joescruggs/bigunderwear.htm</u>. You can even listen to Joe sing a few stanzas in order to catch the tune.

Once the students know the words, you'll prob-

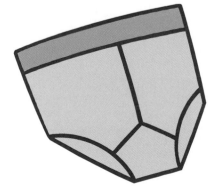

ably want to take a Big Underwear train ride. For more fun, hand out a pair of big boxers to each student before the song (and dancing) begins.

"As Soon as Fred Gets Out of Bed"

Teach students the words to the Jack Prelutsky underwear poem, "As Soon as Fred Gets Out of Bed." It is so funny that they will have an easy time memorizing it in class, but you will want to send home a copy of the words so that family members can learn it, too!

If you have already completed the My Favorite Pair activity, you may want to post the words to the Prelutsky poem on the bulletin board and surround it with pictures of your students' favorite pairs. You can find the words to this poem in *Something BIG Has Been Here* (Greenwillow Books, 1990), or at the poemhunter Web site at <u>www.poemhunter.com/poem/as-soon-as-fred-gets-out-of-bed</u>.

The Umbrella

by Jan Brett. G. P. Putnam's Sons, 2004.

In this Costa Rican Monteverde Cloud Forest version of *The Mitten* (also by Jan Brett), tropical animals make themselves at home in Carlos's upturned leafy green umbrella. The tiny tree frog that hops into the drip-drop puddle is followed by a fig-eating toucan, a tired kinkajou, a lost baby tapir, a proud quetzal, a frisky monkey, a pouncing jaguar, and finally, a tiny little hummingbird who tips the umbrella over—causing everyone to tumble out. Meanwhile, Carlos, up in the giant fig tree, misses it all.

Umbrellas

Invite students to bring in their own umbrellas and stage an umbrella parade around the perimeter of the school or school yard.

Now, place the open, up-ended umbrellas in a circle. Which umbrella could hold the most animals? Which could hold the fewest? Which is the deepest? Which is the shallowest? Are there any umbrellas that are the right color so that an animal could hide in it and be camouflaged? If so, which animal would it be?

Design an Umbrella

Ask students to carefully study the construction of Carlos's umbrella. Why is it the perfect umbrella for a boy living in the cloud forest? Now ask what would be the perfect umbrella for them. Invite students to design an umbrella that suits their environment as well as their interests.

Double Bubble

Pair *The Umbrella* with Jan Brett's version of *The Mitten*. After reading both stories aloud and discussing them, create a Venn diagram to compare and contrast the stories. Once children have identified all of the differences in setting and animals, lead them to discuss the structural and conceptual similarities.

"Behold the Bold Umbrellaphant"

Share the delightful poem, "Behold the Bold Umbrellaphant" with your students from:

📖 **Book Pairing:** *Behold the Bold Umbrellaphant: And Other Poems* by Jack Prelutsky, illustrated by Carin Berger. Greenwillow Books, 2006.

Glue the Horn on the Unicorn

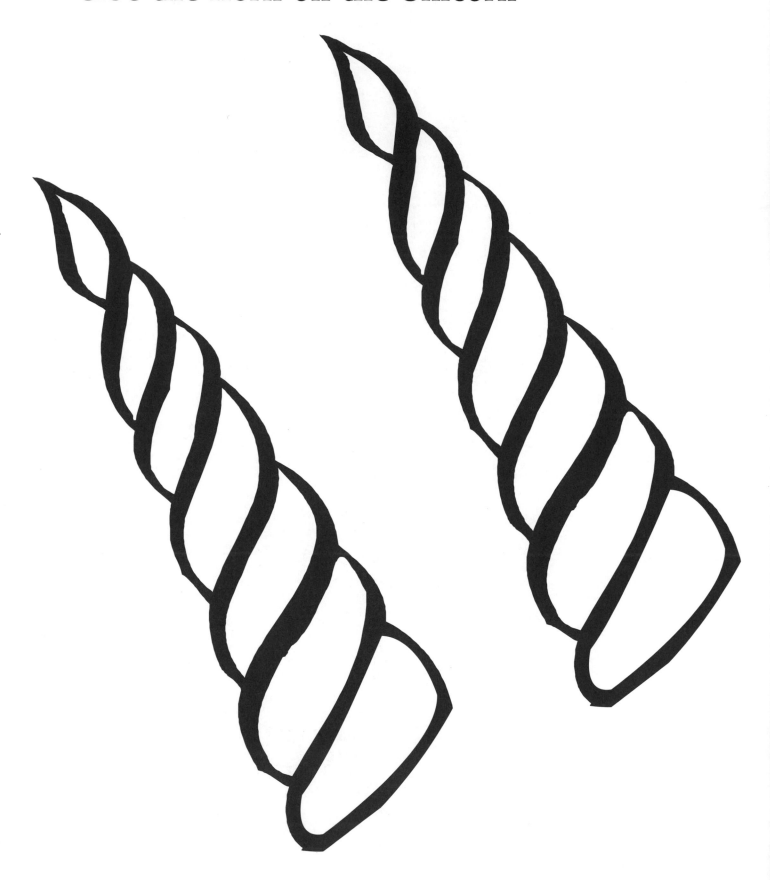

My Favorite Pair

The Ugly Vegetables

by Grace Lin. Talewinds, 1999.

A young Asian American girl celebrates spring by helping her mother to prepare a garden for planting, but they do everything differently from their neighbors. As the flower gardens grow all around, only the narrator's garden is dark green and ugly, but when the vegetables are harvested and made into a delicious soup that fills the neighborhood with an appetizing aroma, the narrator is delighted with the results. And there is plenty to share with the neighbors.

Ugly Vegetable Soup

Author Grace Lin lists the recipe for her Ugly Vegetable Soup at the end of *The Ugly Vegetables*. If you have access to Chinese vegetables in a market near you, gather the ingredients to make this soup with your students.

Vegetable Tasting

Host a vegetable tasting for students. Combine common vegetables like carrots and peppers with more exotic vegetables and Chinese vegetables. Offer them on a platter with toothpicks for sampling.

To extend this as a math activity, graph student favorites.

Many Ugly Vegetables

In the back of *The Ugly Vegetables*, you will find a list of the vegetables that the narrator and her mother grow. The list provides the vegetables' Chinese and English names. Ask students to repeat the names as you read each one aloud, and ask them if the vegetable looks like any vegetables they have seen before.

Now invite students to brainstorm all of the vegetables that they know. When the list is complete, ask them which vegetables they think are ugly, and circle them in dark green. Ask whether they think ugly vegetables can also be delicious.

A Web Visit with Grace Lin

Ask students what it means to pay someone a visit. Are there friends or family members whom they visit often? What do they do when they visit? Have they ever visited a stranger?

Explain that even though Grace Lin, the author/illustrator of *The Ugly Vegetables*, is a stranger, it is possible to visit her by visiting her Web site. In fact, they can see what she looks like, read about her family, and even find out what inspired her to write this book. Now, using a digital projector or an electronic white board, take a visit to Grace Lin's Web site at www.gracelin.com.

Love, Ruby Valentine

by Laurie Friedman, illustrations by Lynne Avril Cravath. Carolrhoda Books, 2006.

Ruby Valentine and Lovebird live deep in the heart of Heartland. Predictably, their favorite holiday is Valentine's Day. They prepare for the big day with much gluing, glittering, rhyming, signing, baking, and wrapping. Sadly, though, the two get so little rest that once all preparations are made, they fall into a deep sleep and miss the holiday entirely. Much to their delight, however, they discover that people love to be loved any day of the year.

Valentine Cards

Whether or not it is Valentine's Day, invite your students to create a Valentine for someone special to them. Provide plenty of paper, glue, glitter, stickers, and curling ribbon.

Valentine Vase

Using the vase template on page 135, cut out enough red and pink vases for each student to have one. Give each student a vase cut-out, a sheet of white paper, several pipe cleaners, a glue stick, and a pair of scissors. Now invite students to decorate their Valentine vases and fill them with as many stemmed hearts and flowers as they like, using cut-out hearts and blossoms, stickers, or hearts and blossoms that they've drawn.

Valentine Venn Diagram

Read another Valentine's Day picture book:

📖 **Book Pairing:** *Roses are Pink, Your Feet Really Stink* by Diane Degroat. HarperCollins, 1997.

Ask students to compare the two stories using a Venn diagram. (Note: You may want to emphasize that Venn also begins with V and that the Venn diagram was introduced by mathematician John Venn in 1881.) Ask students to think about what the holidays are about in the two stories, how the characters prepare, what problems they encounter, and how the dilemma turns out in each case. What similarities and differences do they find when they compare the stories?

Read My Valentine Heart

If possible, purchase a package of Valentine candy conversation hearts for your class. Provide one of the small boxes for each student, or, hand out a three-ounce paper cup full of individual hearts. Begin the activity by asking students to divide their hearts into color piles. Then, ask them to graph their collection by color on a bar graph. Compare results between students.

To extend the activity, ask students to re-divide their candies by slogan, and graph the results again. Additionally, if you have a group of readers or an extra set of eyes, you can create a bingo game for group play with various heart sayings on the squares.

The House Takes a Vacation

by Jacqueline Davies, illustrated by Lee White. Marshall Cavendish, 2007.

When the Petersons leave on vacation, their house decides to get away on a trip too. However, the various components (doors, windows, roof, etc.) disagree on a destination until the sunporch mentions the sea and off they go. When the house attempts to wade in the water at the beach, it is swept out to sea and pointed to shore by a dismissive lighthouse. The Petersons arrive home to find their house back on its sunburned basement, but to their puzzlement, things look a little odd all the way around!

The Perfect Vacation

Reread *The House Takes a Vacation*. Ask students why the house decided to go to the sea. Now invite students to talk about times when any of them has taken a vacation near water, whether the water was an ocean, a lake, or a river. What does the sunporch mean by the Dance of the Sunlight?

Begin by watching a few short videos that capture the natural image of sunlight sparkling on water, such as these on YouTube:

www.youtube.com/watch?v=KMxI-IiL5UU

www.youtube.com/watch?v=4S0SgTaHYe8

Then, invite them to create their own image of the Dance of the Sunlight with paper and paint, or markers. Allow them to add occasional touches of glitter glue for sparkles in the water.

Where Would You Go?

Ask students how many of them have ever been on a vacation. If raised hands are plentiful, ask where they have been on their trips. In order to ensure that everyone has a turn, tell them that today, everyone is going to take an imaginary vacation to a spot they've always wanted to visit. It can be the home of a friend or relative, a place they have heard of but never visited, or a familiar spot that they would like to return to once more.

Give students some quiet time to reflect on their destination. Then, ask them to close their eyes and imagine how they feel in that place. Invite each student to complete the following sentence:

I went to _____, and while I was there I felt _____.

Explain that "happy" might be a common emotion, but ask them to stretch further and find other adjectives to express their feelings, such as excited, bubbly, or surprised.

Take a Visiting Vacation

Sometimes the best vacations happen when you go for a visit to see someone you love and whom you haven't seen for a long time. Begin by sharing a book about just such a trip:

📖 **Book Pairing:** *The Relatives Came* by Cynthia Rylant, illustrated by Stephen Gammell. Atheneum, 2001.

Then ask students to talk about times when they have gone on a vacation to visit someone. What were the best parts? What memories were created?

Views from Vacation

Ask your students to pretend that they are some component of the house that takes a vacation. Their assignment is to create a postcard to send home to the Petersons. Have a stack of picture postcards on hand to familiarize students with a typical postcard design, and to provide inspiration.

Discuss which house component each child would like to become, what they will picture on the front of their postcard, and what they will write on the reverse. Then, hand out oaktag cards cut to oversize postcard size, and invite them to design their own cards.

Valentine Vase

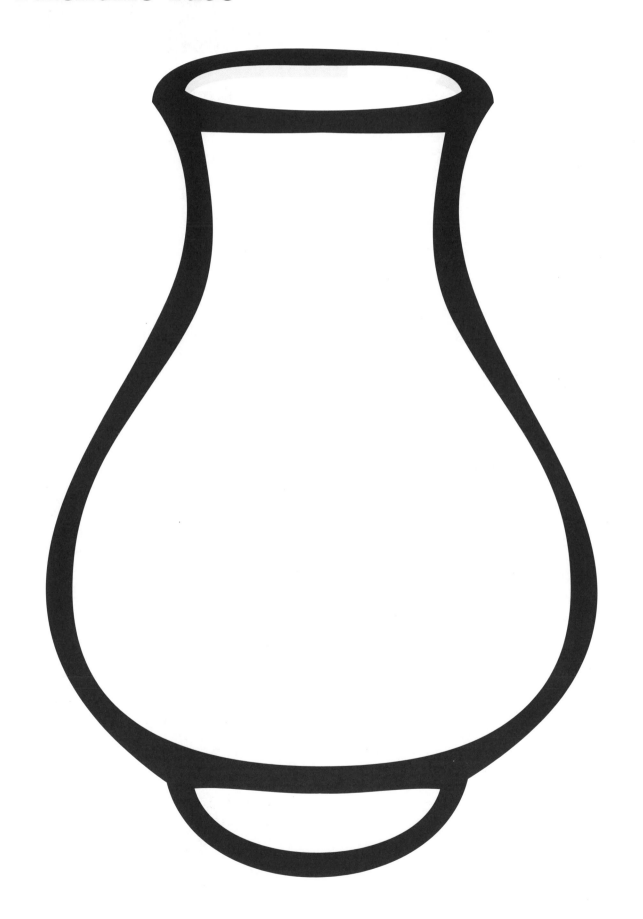

Winter is the Warmest Season

by Lauren Stringer. Harcourt, 2006.

In first-person narrative, the young protagonist convincingly argues that winter is the warmest season, despite logic to the contrary. Contrasting the cozy warmth of radiators, laps, fireplaces, candles, winter clothing, winter activities, and winter food and drink with the coolness of summer foods and swimming pools, the protagonist builds a persuasive and compelling case.

Winter Impressions

Before reading *Winter is the Warmest Season* aloud to the class, ask them to brainstorm winter words that come to mind. Create a web of these words on chart paper. Write the word WINTER in the center of the web, and draw spokes from the center all around it at varying lengths. At the end of each spoke, draw a circle and write a student word within it. After the winter word web is complete, read the web aloud to students and ask them to decide whether each word is a warm or cold concept. Use a stamp or freehand drawing (perhaps of a sun and a snowflake) to label each word appropriately. Alternately, use red for warm and blue for cold and retrace the circle surrounding each word in color.

Add the words that you have generated to a winter word wall on which you have posted a series of oaktag rectangles with words printed in large, bold letters. Note that some teachers and librarians mount words in alphabetical order.

Warm in Winter

Before reading *Winter is the Warmest Season* aloud to the class, ask students what they think the author might mean by the title. How can winter be the warmest season? Then read, looking for clues. After reading, ask them to generate a list of warm winter things that the narrator talks about in the story. List them and ask students to explain why each item is "warm" in winter.

Next, compare each warm winter item in the book to your winter word web. Are all of the concepts on your web? If not, add them. If they are, are they labeled "warm" on your web? If not, what made the class label them cold, instead?

Wintry Poems

Begin by sharing a selection of wintry poems with the class. The CanTeach Web site has an extensive collection at www.canteach.ca/elementary/songspoems7.html. After sharing these poems and discussing individual favorites, invite students to first create a simple class poem using the words on the winter word web you have created. Then, once students are comfortable with poetry creation, ask them to create individual short poems. If needed, have older student "scribes" on hand to record the young students' poems.

Opposite Seasons

Invite students to notice how often author Lauren Stringer contrasts a winter idea with a summer idea. Re-read the book and record each contrasting seasonal idea on a Venn diagram for all to see. Now, ask students to think of more opposites that pertain to the two seasons in places where winter is cold and summer is hot. If you live in a warm climate, you might want to engage in an activity that focuses on the similarities between the two seasons by having a large overlap in your two circles.

Wiggle

by Doreen Cronin, illustrated by Scott Menchin. Atheneum, 2005.

Although the text of this book begins with the alarm clock rousing the wiggly dog protagonist and ends with him snoozing atop his doghouse under a crescent moon, this is more of a poem and activity book than a story. In a series of funny questions, author Doreen Cronin encourages kids to wiggle in many ways and with many objects and animals. Be prepared to wiggle when you read this book!

Wigglefest

Stage a wigglefest for your young listeners on the day that you read *Wiggle*. You can find two wiggle rhymes to teach them at the Toronto Public Library KidsSpace Printables page at kidsspace.torontopubliclibrary.ca/Offline%20Activities/documents/rhymes_openclose.pdf.

Wiggles and Sillies

Combine all the fun of *Wiggles* with the hilarity of shaking your sillies out with a companion book (and song):

📖 **Book Pairing:** *Shake My Sillies Out* by Raffi, illustrated by David Allender. Crown Publishers, 1990.

Play a recording of Raffi singing the song, encouraging students to join the singing and motions. If you do not own the *Raffi in Concert* CD, listen to Raffi sing the song online at the Rhapsody Online site at www.rhapsody.com/raffi/inconcert/shakemysilliesout/lyrics.html.

Who Else Wiggles?

Challenge students to think of animals in the natural world who wiggle. Make a list of all of their ideas. Now ask them to search their list for animals who wiggle and whose names start with W. If there isn't a W animal on your list, ask them to think of one. Once students have come up with worm as the W wiggling animal, share the story of Wiggle and Waggle:

📖 **Book Pairing:** *Wiggle and Waggle* by Caroline Arnold, illustrated by Mary Peterson. Charlesbridge, 2007.

You will find an extensive teachers guide to this book at the TeacherVision Web site at www.teachervision.fen.com/tv/printables/charlesbridge/charlesbridge_WiggleWaggle.pdf.

We Wiggle Too

Ask your physical education teacher to join you in the library or classroom on *Wiggle* day, or ask if you can host your *Wiggle* read-aloud in the gym. Ask the physical education instructor to teach students to use hula hoops in a controlled wiggle, just as the main character of *Wiggle* does on the cover of the book. Give students time to practice with the hoops.

Now spread out and practice wiggling like each of the animals in the book: fish, crocodile, bee, polar bear, snake, and chick. Ask them to think of other animals and then, as a group, wiggle like each one.

Waiting for Wings

by Lois Ehlert. Harcourt, 2001.

With staged paper sizes, Ehlert relates the story of the butterfly life cycle from hidden eggs, to hatching caterpillars, to chrysalises, to winged butterflies that head for the sky in search of nectar-laden flowers. As the insects grow from tiny eggs to full-size butterflies, the pages, illustrations, and font size increase right along with them. Ultimately, the rhyming, lilting text and boldly-colored illustrations take those butterflies right back to the fields from whence they came—this time, to lay their own eggs!

Wings to Fly

Read through *Waiting for Wings* a few times to be certain that students understand the sequence of the events described in the book. Then, ask students to relate the events, one at a time, by completing the following statement:

The _____ (what?) are in the _____ (where?) _____ (doing what?).

Once you are satisfied with the statements, create a set of sentence strips and practice putting them in order using a sentence strip pocket chart. Remind students that the title tells them that WINGS come later in the story.

Getting to Wings

Ask students to review the process a butterfly undergoes during its life cycle by identifying each step that is outlined in *Waiting for Wings*. Once you have reviewed the process, ask students to complete the Getting to Wings graphic organizer (see page 140) by making four drawings. You may want to enlarge the organizer to give your students more room to draw.

What Flies?

The end of *Waiting for Wings* includes a "Butterfly Identification" spread. After studying it and matching those butterflies up to the illustrations in the second half of the book, ask students to brainstorm other insects with wings. Create a list of them. Next, ask students to brainstorm a list of other animals with wings. Finally, ask them to brainstorm a list of non-living things with wings.

Ask each student to review the lists and choose one insect, one animal, and one non-animal with wings to illustrate on the What Flies graphic organizer (see page 141).

"Butterfly Wings"

Share the beautiful poem by Aileen Fisher entitled "Butterfly Wings" with your students. You can find the text of the poem, as well as several curriculum activities, at the Scholastic in the Classroom Web site at teacher.scholastic.com/lessonrepro/lessonplans/profbooks/butterwings.pdf.

Water Hole Waiting

**by Jane Kurtz and Christopher Kurtz,
illustrated by Lee Christiansen.
Greenwillow Books, 2002.**

Mama and Monkey spend a long and thirsty day on the savannah, from the moment morning licks up the night shadows, until evening sighs and the sun sinks. The sun is hot all day, and Monkey is impatient to make his way to the tempting water hole. But Mama knows better, and each time she grabs him, she saves him from certain danger posed by other, bigger animals visiting the water hole. At last, as crickets start their chirping, Monkey wiggles all the way down to the water hole and drinks.

Water on the Savannah

Once you have shared *Water Hole Waiting* with the class, ask students to talk about what they know about water holes and savannahs from reading this book. You might draw on potential knowledge of water holes and savannahs from those who have seen *The Lion King*.

Ask students to name some of the activities that happen at the water hole. (Note: encourage children to look closely at the pictures in the book.) Then, share other water hole picture books with students and then ask them to add to what they already know about the savannah and the water hole:

📖 **Book Pairing:** *Chubbo's Pool* by Betsy Lewin. Clarion Books, 1995.

Who Comes? by Deborah Chandra, illustrated by Katie Lee. Sierra Club, 1995.

Monkey Waits

From the time the sun rises, Monkey is impatient to get to the water hole for a drink. But Mama is much more cautious. Each time he tries to go, she captures him by one of his body parts and keeps him with her.

Ask students to complete the following sentences for each event in the story:

Monkey _____ (what does he do?).

Wait! Mama grabs his _____.

_____ is at the water hole.

Now invite them to choose their favorite sentences and illustrate them.

You Wait, Too

No doubt your students feel quite a bit like Monkey sometimes. They also have to wait and WAIT and WAIT for what they want—and what they want to do.

Initiate a conversation with the class about things they have to wait for and things they have to wait to do. Generate two labeled lists, and write down the students' ideas. Once the lists are complete, ask students to consider the reasons they have to wait for each thing. Draw a bold circle around the things they have to wait for because there is danger involved, as there is for Monkey.

Your Own Water Hole

Invite students to help you create your very own classroom water hole on the bulletin board. From paper, create a cool blue pool surrounded by grassland and acacia trees. Then, give students individual sheets of paper and ask each student to draw one or more of its kind. Have students cut them out (you may want to assign older student buddies to help with this) and then place them around the water hole with glue or staples. Finally, put Mama and Monkey off in a tree waiting.

Getting to Wings

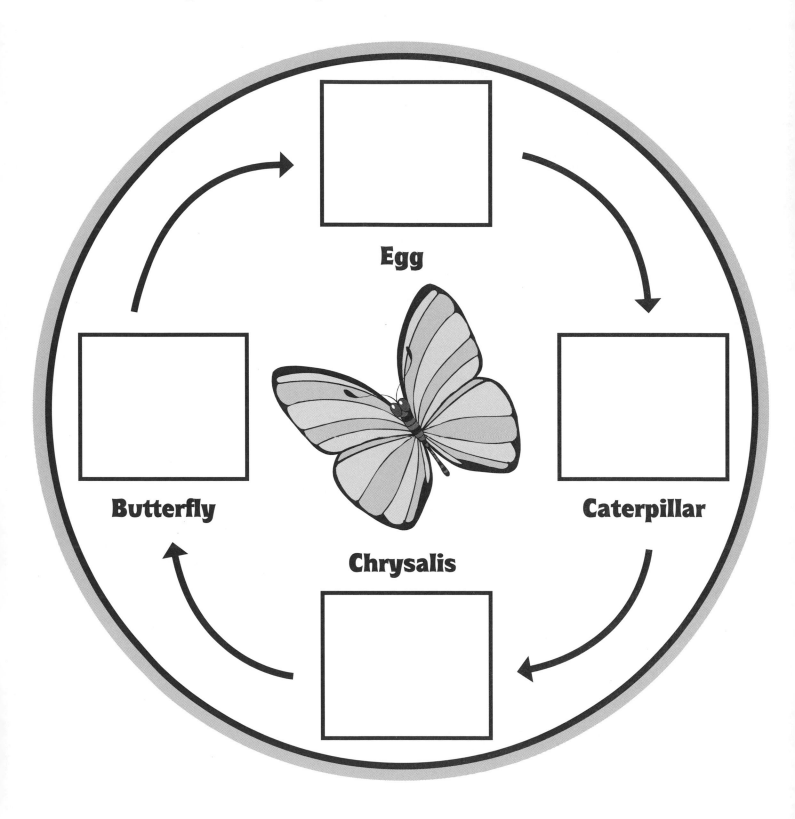

Egg

Caterpillar

Chrysalis

Butterfly

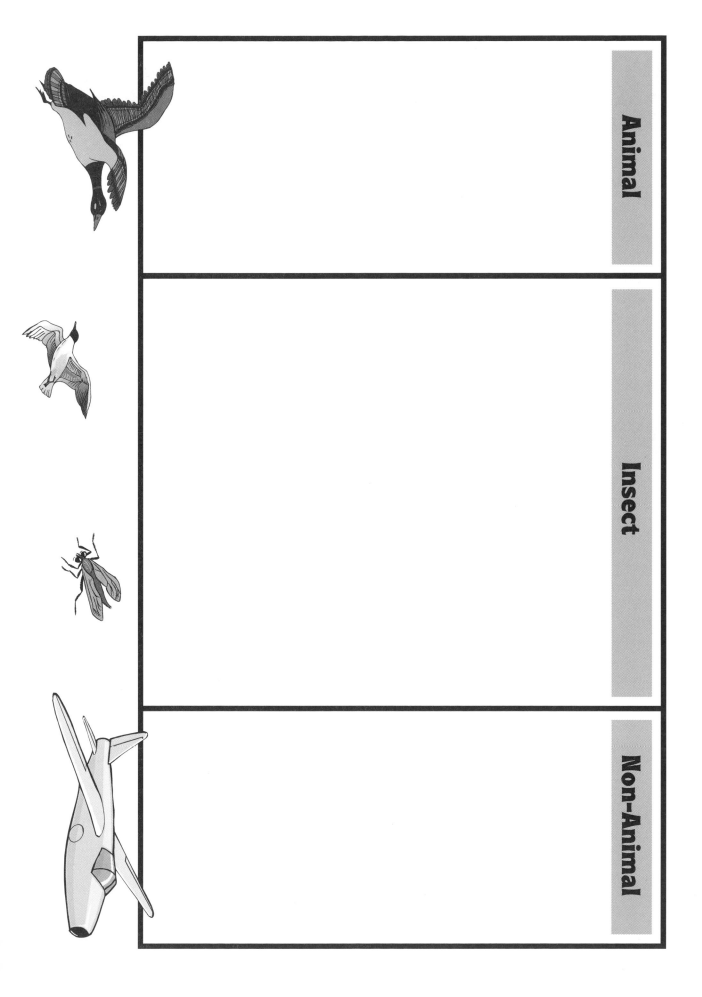

What Flies?

Animal	Insect	Non-Animal

Jessica's X-Ray

by Pat Zonta, illustrated by Clive Dobson. Firefly Books, 2002.

Jessica's once-perfect day is ruined when she falls out of a tree and breaks her arm. She is whisked to Children's Hospital, where Doctor Dave orders an x-ray. Jessica, the narrator, talks about her fears, but reassures the reader that getting an x-ray is completely painless. Interleaved acetate pages show x-rays, a CAT-scan, a prenatal ultrasound, and an MRI of the head. These pages include questions to guide the interpretation of each image. Answers are provided at the end of the book, along with a general Q&A.

What's Inside?

Begin by explaining that x-rays allow us to see bones inside the human body. Discuss the purpose of these bones. Have students stand up, and ask them to imagine what would happen if various bones in their bodies were missing, one at a time:

- What if the bones in your hands were missing?

- What if the bones in your neck were missing?

- What if the bones in your arms were missing?

- What if the bones in your legs were missing? (Instruct students to sink down carefully.)

Now share a book about how the bones in the body are connected.

📖 **Book Pairing:** *Dem Bones* by Bob Barner. Chronicle Books, 1996.

Teach your students the spiritual upon which *Dem Bones* is based with students. Find a Blues version of the song at the Brownie Locks Web site at www.brownielocks.com/dembones.html.

Take an X-ray

Ask students to look closely at the x-ray of a six-year-old child's hand. Show them the two places near the wrist where Jessica's arm is broken. Now ask them to look closely at how the bones in her hand and fingers look. Point out the joints in the fingers.

Trace each child's hand with chalk on a dark piece of construction paper. Ask them to imagine that they are taking an x-ray of that hand with an x-ray machine. Using chalk, ask them to draw in the bones of their hands.

Animal Bones

X-rays can make pictures of people's bones as well as animals' bones. Share the x-rays of animal bones that you will find on the X-ray for Kids Web site at www.uhrad.com/kids.htm.

As you project each x-ray with a digital projector (click the x-ray to get an individual view of it), ask students to guess what the animal is and to provide reasons for their responses.

Boney or Boneless?

Play the Boney or Boneless game with your students on the Children's Museum of Indianapolis' Bones: An Exhibit Inside You Web site at www.childrensmuseum.org/special_exhibits/bones/kids_mazeGame.htm.

EX Words

Before reading *Extra! Extra! Fairy-Tale News from Hidden Forest*, talk about the title of the book. Read it aloud to them. Ask what letter they think "extra" begins with. Now explain that there are several words in our language that sound like they begin with X but which actually begin with EX, as extra does.

Brainstorm other words that begin with an X (ks) sound. As students contribute words, write them down in one of two columns, one labeled with an X and one labeled with an EX.

Samples of other EX words that young students might know are excitement, exit, exercise, example, and extinct.

Our Newspaper Extra

Explain to students that an "extra" in newspaper terms is an additional issue of the newspaper, usually printed to report an uncommon or critical event. Ask if they know why one issue of the *Hidden Forest International* in *Extra! Extra! Fairy-Tale News from Hidden Forest* is published as an extra. What are the surprising and possibly dangerous events that the extra issue covers?

Now challenge students to create their own extra for the school bulletin or newspaper. Allow them to decide on a single alarming or uncommon event to write about, or have them choose a variety of events to cover. Give each student a column's width of paper on which to draw and/or draw and write about the event of their choice.

Assemble the "articles" into an extra edition of the news.

Extras in Math

Give students a set of cards with numbering 1–10 (or 20, depending on mathematical knowledge), along with 11 (or 21) Cuisenaire® or other manipulative blocks. Ask students to choose a card and count out the number of blocks indicated on the card, plus one extra. If you have previously introduced odd and even numbers, you may wish to use this activity to emphasize the way in which one extra transforms odd to even and even to odd.

"Extra! Extra! Special News"

Teach students the lyrics to this song, sung to the tune of "Twinkle, Twinkle, Little Star."

"Extra! Extra! Special News"

Extra! Extra! Special news.

Hidden Forest had to choose.

Giant beanstalk growing high.

Climbing up into the sky.

Extra! Extra! What to do?

Chop the beanstalk where it grew.

What Do Babies Eat?

Begin by asking the class to list all of the foods that each of the babies in the story ate. Ask whether or not they agree with the yuck/yum assessment that is given to each food. Why? Ask them to think more deeply about why that particular meal would be unappealing or appealing. You may want to suggest that they begin each statement in this way:

I would like/dislike eating a _____ because it would be _____ and _____.

Ask students to be as specific as possible. (This activity teaches the use of details in speaking, and, eventually, writing.)

Marked for Exclamation

Explain that exclamatory words are words that have no independent meaning other than to express an emotion. Ask students what the two exclamatory words are in the book, *Yuck!*

Ask them to notice that each of the exclamations is accompanied by an exclamation mark. What work do they think the exclamation mark does? Lead them in a discussion of the purpose of the exclamation mark. Practice, in pairs, saying "Yuck" with and without an exclamation point. Practice again with "Yum."

Exclaiming!

"Yuck!" and "Yum!" are two exclamatory words that begin with Y. Ask students to make a list of other exclamatory words, trying to add additional Y exclamations to the list. Whenever a student suggests a word beginning with Y, change the color of the marker you are using and make that Y a bright red, to emphasize the word.

Now, share another book featuring exclamations with the class:

📖 **Book Pairing:** *Yikes!!!* by Robert Florczak. Blue Sky Press, 2003.

Ask students to list the exclamatory words in the book. If they are already on your list, underline them with blue. If there are new Y words, again write that word with a bright red Y.

"Apples Are Yummy"

Teach students the song below, sung to the tune of "Frère Jacques." After singing the song the way it is written, invite students to change the words to include other foods. For even more fun, let them pretend they are baby animals and sing lines such as "Worms are yummy!"

Apples are yummy.

Pears are yummy.

Blueberries too.

Strawberries too.

I will taste what you like.

You can taste what I like.

I'll share with you.

I'll share with you.

YUMMY!

> ### *Yo! Yes?*
>
> **by Chris Raschka. Orchard Books, 1993.**
>
> Told in a very few words, this is the story of a new friendship between a white boy and an African American boy who meet on the street. The African American boy approaches the white boy in a friendly, open, and persistent exchange. When the white boy finally admits to having "no friends," the other boy offers his friendship and the white boy accepts in a moment of giggling joy.

On Stage

Begin by reading the book aloud several times, enabling pre-readers to learn the pattern of the story and some of the language. Then, invite students to take turns, in pairs, enacting this short text. Make large cue cards for each character in two different colors. Then, begin with Boy One's first turn to speak. Hold up his first cue card, which reads "Yo!" Next, hold up Boy Two's cue card, which reads "Yes?" Alternate cue cards and encourage students to both read the words and use the body language they see in the illustrations on each page. (Note: If you have a document camera,

this would be an excellent time to project the book on a screen.)

Just a Few Words

Students will notice that this book has far fewer words than most picture books. Discuss why that might be. Point out to students that they actually know quite a bit about what is going on in the story with only these few words.

Now, invite them to expand the text on each page while you act as their scribe. As you share each character's dialogue, ask students what he means. For instance, on the first page, the character says, "Yo!" What is another way that he might have said this? Might he have said, "Hello?" Might he have said, "Hey, you?" Continue through the story, writing down the alternate dialogue. Then read it through as you turn the pages of the book, so that students can combine the new text while experiencing the illustrations.

Finally, ask them which text they think worked best and discuss the reasons why.

Start with a Y

There are many Y words in the text of *Yo! Yes?* Ask students to help you to make a list of all of them. Then, invite students to add to your list by including other Y words they can think of. For each word they add, ask them if it could have been said by a character in this story, in a one- or two-word line. If the answer is yes, circle that word in green. Discuss what the character might be asking or telling by using that word.

Yes Sir!

For fun, invite your kids to join you in singing "Baa, Baa, Black Sheep."

Baa, baa, black sheep,

Have you any wool?

Yes sir, yes sir,

Three bags full.

One for the master,

One for the dame,

And one for the little boy

Who lives down the lane.

Baa, baa, black sheep,

Have you any wool?

Yes sir, yes sir,

Three bags full.

If you are not familiar with the tune, you can listen to it on the Kiddles Web site at <www.kididdles.com/lyrics/b001.html>.

The Happiest Tree: A Yoga Story

by Uma Krishnaswami, illustrated by Ruth Jeyaveeran. Lee & Low Books, 2005.

At first, Meena is excited about the class play—a re-telling of *Red Riding Hood*. But after spilling the paint while decorating the set, she is upset to learn that she has to have a part in the play. She feels too clumsy for that. When Mrs. Vohra, owner of the Indian grocery, encourages Meena to join the children's yoga class, she agrees. Yoga teaches her a way to quiet her body's movements and to successfully play a quiet tree in Red Riding Hood's forest.

Yoga

After reading *The Happiest Tree: A Yoga Story* aloud to the class, ask how many students have practiced yoga in the past. If you have some students who have, ask whether they can remember any of the poses they learned. If so, ask them to name and demonstrate the pose. Use a nonfiction yoga book to identify the pose, such as:

📖 **Book Pairing:** *I Love Yoga* by Mary Kaye Chryssicas, illustrated by Angela Coppola. DK, 2005.

(Note: You may want to team up with your physical education teacher as you extend the learning from *The Happiest Tree: A Yoga Story*.)

Be a Tree

The yoga pose that Meena learns that is most helpful to her in performing in *Red Riding Hood* is called the Tree pose. Visit the ABC-of-Yoga online at www.abc-of-yoga.com/yoga-practice/tree-yoga-pose.asp to see an animated enactment of the pose. Teach your kids the tree pose based on instructions found at this site or in *The Happiest Tree*. If time allows, invite your students to create a tree costume such as Meena's in the book or the more elaborate one on YogaKids.

Meena's Yoga Poses

In the afterword to *The Happiest Tree*, Jeyaveeran illustrates the four other yoga poses that Meena learns in her class, in addition to the Tree pose. Teach students each of the four poses (Frog, Lotus, Cat, Cobra) by referring to *I Love Yoga* again or another yoga book for kids such as:

📖 **Book Pairing:** *Yoga Bear: Yoga for Youngsters* by Karen Pierce, illustrated by Paula Brinkman. NorthWord Press, 2004.

Yoga Poems

Begin by practicing some yoga poses. Then, read some yoga poems for children aloud to the class from:

📖 **Book Pairing:** *Twist: Yoga Poems* by Janet S. Wong, illustrated by Julie Paschkis. Margaret K. McElderry Books, 2007.

Now, invite the class to focus on one pose that you have learned and practiced together. Capture images from the pose in words or phrases. Write these on the board or chart and then work with students to fashion them into a poem.

Zara Zebra Counts

by Brigitte Weninger, illustrated by Anna Laura Cantone. North-South Books, 2002.

Zara Zebra has some candy. She doesn't know how much she has, but it is certainly too much for one little zebra. She invites her friend bear to share, but it's still too much. When Duck and Crocodile join them, they still have too much candy. At last, they ask Kitty to join them. Finally, they have the perfect number of friends for the five pieces of candy.

Zillions of Zebras

Ask students what they find most interesting about zebras. No doubt, someone will mention the zebra's stripes. Introduce the topic of animal adaptations. Tell them that fish have gills so that they can live underwater. Birds have hollow bones so that they can fly. Now ask them if they know why zebras have stripes. It may be a difficult one to guess.

Share an image of a herd of zebras such as the one at the BBC Web site at news.bbc.co.uk/1/hi/sci/tech/4501052.stm to help them to understand the advantage of the adaptation.

Stripe the Zebra

Give each student an unstriped zebra cutout (see template on page 151), a glue stick, and a handful of black construction paper strips. Tell them that this zebra is not adapted for life in the wild with his fellow zebras, and that he must have some stripes. When the zebras are completed, create a savannah mural with tall grass, a few acacia trees, and, off to the side, a hungry lion. Now, ask students to come up

to the mural, one by one, to create a herd of striped zebras. Instruct them to be sure that the zebras are standing in front of, next to, and behind each other, so that individual outlines disappear from the sight of that hungry lion.

Zero to a Zillion

Ask students how many pieces of candy Zara Zebra had. When they respond "five," ask them what the letter "five" begins with. Now challenge them to think of two numbers that begin with Z. It will be interesting to discuss the mathematical meanings of these two words with students. While zero is a number you can't count, because it means none, it is a real number, whereas zillion is also a number you can't count but that is because it has no definite amount attached to it. It simply indicates a very large number.

Now, give each student a sheet of white paper and a marker. Ask them to make zero dots on their page. All pages will remain blank. Now, give them a specific amount of minutes and ask them to try to make a zillion dots on the page with the marker. When time is called, ask if anyone has a zillion. When students answer affirmatively, explain that no one actually has a zillion dots, because if you were to count all the dots, you would get to a definite number.

"I Dreamed I Was Riding a Zebra"

Share this funny poem by Kenn Nesbitt with your students. It can be found at the Poetry4Kids Web site at www.poetry4kids.com/poem-72.html. They will easily memorize it because of the memorable visual images it includes. Once they are able to recite it aloud, you may want to stage a recitation. If you have time, have students use the Stripe the Zebra template on page 151 to produce zebras with stripes and pink curly hair mounted on popsicle sticks.

The Animals We've Seen

Challenge students to make a list of all of the animals they read about and see in the illustrations of the book. Using chart paper, create a vertical list of the animals they see. Now, in two columns (labeled At the Zoo and In the Wild), ask students, one animal at a time, to tell you whether they have ever seen this animal, and if so, where—at the zoo or in the wild. Supply checkmarks for each student response and then draw conclusions about the most often-seen animals.

Born Free

Keeping in mind the age and developmental level of your students, conduct a conversation about zoos and captivity of animals. Ask first whether they have ever been to a zoo. Ask next why they think we have zoos. Next ask whether they think animals would rather be in the zoo or in the wild. Remind them of the story in *Never, EVER Shout in a Zoo*. Ask them why they think the animals might have wanted to escape and why they might have locked the people up. Take care to look at the positive aspects of zoos as well, and to leave students thinking about both sides of the issue without feeling overwhelmed.

"I See Animals"

Sing this song to the tune of "Frère Jacques." Once you have sung the first three verses, ask students to add verses for the many animals who continue to join the chase (hippos, lions, tigers, kangaroos, snakes, flamingos, crocodiles), and all of the other animals they have spotted in the illustrations of the stampede.

"I See Animals"

I see grizzly bears.
I see grizzly bears.

In the zoo.
In the zoo.

Never shout around them.
Never shout around them.

They'll chase you.
They'll chase you.

I see bull moose.
I see bull moose.

In the zoo.
In the zoo.

Never shout around them.
Never shout around them.

They'll chase, too.
They'll chase, too.

I see clever apes.
I see clever apes.

In the zoo.
In the zoo.

Never shout around them.
Never shout around them.

They'll chase, too.
They'll chase, too.

What Comes Next?

Challenge students to create the sequel to *Never, EVER Shout in a Zoo*. What happens if you shout right next to the new exhibit of the dinosaur frozen in ice? Encourage students to think about the pattern in the original story, and, of course, to keep the setting at the zoo! Or, you might like to re-create the current story but set it at the aquarium or the museum. Be sure to discuss the sorts of animals that would be present at these alternate locations.

Zoom!

By Robert Munsch, illustrated by Michael Martchenko. Scholastic Cartwheel, 2003.

Lauretta heads off to try out new wheelchairs at the store. She deems each one she tries to be too slow until she spots the ninety-two speed black, silver, and red dirt-bike chair. The shop owner allows her to take it home for a day's trial. Because the chair is so fast, her brother advises her to drive on the road, which earns her a hundred dollar speeding ticket. However, when her brother injures himself, the wheelchair gets him to the hospital in time.

Zooming

Begin by discussing the verb "zoom" with your students. Solicit their definitions of the word. Then, share the definition of "zoom" from a good primary dictionary such as *Merriam-Webster's Primary Dictionary* by Ruth Heller (2005). If students are familiar with the use of the dictionary, ask them where they think you might find the word "zoom" in the dictionary to reinforce their location skills.

Now, explain that disabled athletes can sometimes zoom as fast as or even faster than those without disabilities. For instance, athletes in wheelchairs can sometimes finish a marathon almost an hour faster than those running on their legs. And athletes in specially outfitted wheelchairs can travel up to fifty-plus miles per hour on rocky mountain trails. Discuss whether Lauretta might want to get involved in sports for kids in wheelchairs. Ask students to support their claims that she would or would not want to be involved.

What Zooms?

Challenge kids to create a list of living and non-living things that zoom. You might want to start the list with Lauretta's wheelchair. If you are in the midst of learning about living and non-living things, you may want to label two columns with those words and identify each listed item by one of those two categories. Or,

you might want to create a vehicle and non-vehicle list.

Once you have a lengthy list, ask students to choose one item to illustrate on drawing paper. Create a bulletin board or wall display labeled "What Zooms?" from their illustrations.

Zoom Lens

Discuss homophones with the class (two words that are spelled the same—and may be pronounced the same—but have different meanings). After sharing a few simple examples (fair/fair, well/well, mine/mine), discuss the word "zoom" as a homophone. Ask what the word means in the title and text of the book, *Zoom!*

Now, discuss the zoom action of a lens of a camera. If you have a digital camera in the school, bring it in to demonstrate the action of zooming. Share two wordless picture books that work on the concept of zooming.

📖 **Book Pairing:** *Zoom* by Istvan Banyai. Viking, 1995.

Re-Zoom by Istvan Banyai. Viking, 1995.

"Zippety, Zappety, Zoom"

Teach students to sing "Hickory, Dickory, Dock!" You can find lyrics and a midi-file for the original song at the National Institutes of Health, Department of Health & Human Services Web site at kids.niehs.nih.gov/lyrics/hickory.htm. Now, sing "Zippety Zappety Zoom" to the same tune.

If your students would like to continue the song, challenge them to write verses 7–12.

"Zippety, Zappety, Zoom"

Zippety, zappety, zoom.
The chair sails round the room.
The clock strikes one.
Her shoelace is undone.
Zippety, zappety, zoom.

Zippety, zappety, zoom.
The chair sails round the room.
The clock strikes two.
She ties her shoe.
Zippety, zappety, zoom.

Zippety, zappety, zoom.
The chair sails round the room.
The clock strikes three.
She's on a spree.
Zippety, zappety, zoom.

Zippety, zappety, zoom.
The chair sails round the room.
The clock strikes four.
She crashes the door.
Zippety, zappety, zoom.

Zippety, zappety, zoom.
The chair sails round the room.
The clock strikes five.
She swoops and dives.
Zippety, zappety, zoom.

Zippety, zappety, zoom.
The chair sails round the room.
The clock strikes six.
She's got more tricks.
Zippety, zappety, zoom.

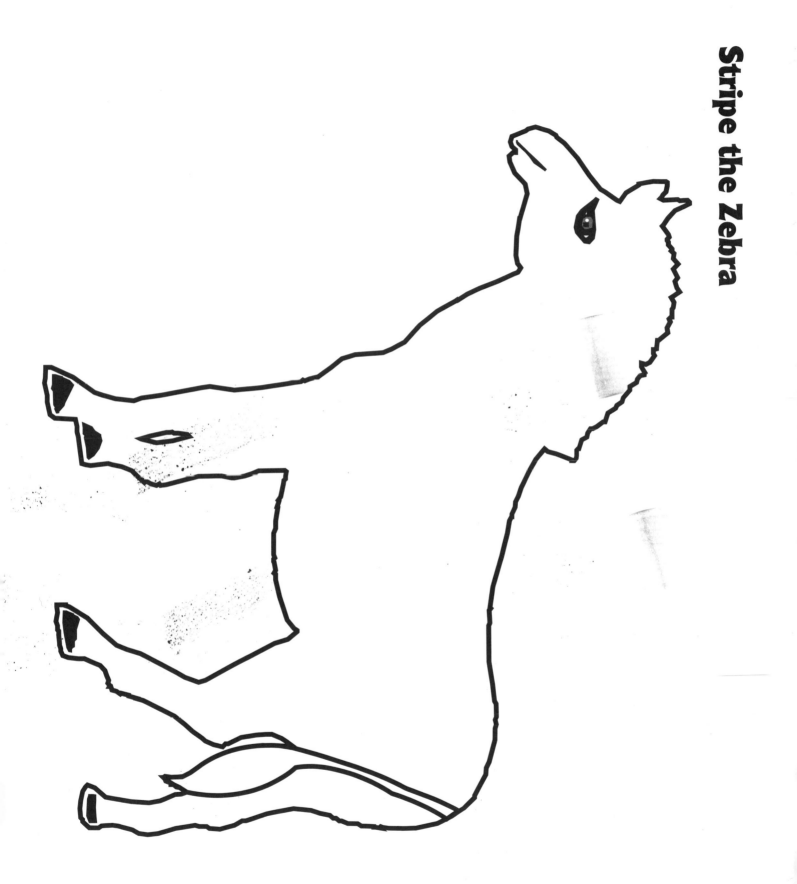